SINS OF THE PRESS

THE UNTOLD STORY OF THE BOSTON GLOBE'S REPORTING ON SEX ABUSE IN THE CATHOLIC CHURCH

DAVID F. PIERRE, JR.
Mattapoisett, Massachusetts

First revised edition

ISBN-13: 978-1511852593
ISBN-10: 1511852593

Printed in the United States of America

CONTENTS

Introduction

Victims are rightfully angered because of the immense betrayal and harm inflicted upon them by criminal priests. The damage inflicted upon innocent youth is immeasurable.

John J. Geoghan, Joseph Birmingham, Ronald Paquin … the list of shameful priests goes on. They are men who never should have been admitted into the priesthood in the first place.

The incessant and fevered reporting of the abuse scandals by the *Boston Globe*, however, is an entirely different matter.

Beginning with its first article on Sunday, January 6, 2002, the *Globe* reaped universal praise for its exhaustive coverage of how the Archdiocese of Boston dealt with cases of priests who were accused of sexually harming minors. Even many reputable Catholic journalists lauded the paper for its work. And in April 2003, the *Globe* and its Spotlight Team, the investigative arm of the paper that carried out the story, scored a much-coveted Pulitzer Prize for their efforts.

In truth, however, one cannot imagine a newspaper more hypocritical and biased than the *Boston Globe* to report on the issue of sex abuse.

This book shows that whether it be celebrating child molesters or ignoring child sex abuse just steps from its offices, the *Globe* was hardly concerned with the atrocious abuse of minors until it saw that it was a useful cudgel with which it could browbeat the Catholic Church.

Close to a dozen times in its paper over the years, the *Globe* enthusiastically touted a sex education book written by an author who actually praised incest between fathers and daughters, claiming that such acts could be both "satisfying" and "enriching." Unbelievably, the *Globe* recommended this author to children as young as 12.

The *Globe* has even gone as far as to endorse a politician for United States Congress even *after* he publicly admitted to repeatedly having sex with a high school boy.

This book will also expose how the *Globe*'s reporting was simply the culmination of a decades-long crusade of animus against the Catholic Church. This book provides several examples of the paper's bigotry against the Church as shown in numerous articles and editorial cartoons.

The *Globe*'s prejudiced attacks on the Church over the years are legion, such as the time when homosexual activists pelted young priests and their families with condoms and obscenities outside an ordination ceremony, yet the *Globe* merely reported the episode as "peaceful."

Indeed, in April 2003, fifteen months after the paper's incessant reporting began, a *Globe* columnist essentially admitted that her paper had been openly engaged in a "war" with the Catholic Church.

And part of the *Globe*'s war was its evasive portrayal of Boston Cardinal Bernard Law's handling of the case of John J. Geoghan, one of the Church's most notorious molesters. In its frenetic 2002 reporting, the *Globe* would maintain that

Law's response to revelations of abuse by Geoghan "was simply to sweep Geoghan and his troubles to another parish."[1]

Not even close. One of the most misleading aspects of the *Globe*'s reporting was how the paper routinely minimized the major role that secular psychologists played in the entire Catholic Church abuse scandal. Time after time, trained "expert" psychologists around the country repeatedly insisted to Church leaders that abusive priests were fit to return to ministry after receiving "treatment" under their care.

Tragically, this scenario also played out repeatedly with the case of John Geoghan and Cardinal Law.

And it is not as if the *Globe* could plead ignorance to the fact that the Church had for years been sending abusive priests to therapy and returning them to ministry on the advice of doctors. In 1992 – a full decade before the *Globe* vented its heralded onslaught against the Church – the paper was enthusiastically promoting in its pages the psychological treatment of sex offenders, including Catholic priests, as "highly effective" and "dramatic."

The *Globe knew* that the Church's practice of sending abusive priests off to treatment was not just some diabolical attempt to deflect responsibility and cover up wrongdoing, but a genuine attempt to treat aberrant priests that was being widely promoted by secular experts in the field.

Yet ten years later, in 2002, the *Globe* acted in mock horror that the Church had employed such treatments. It bludgeoned the Church for doing in 1992 exactly what the *Globe* itself said it should be doing. The hypocrisy is off the charts.

Indeed, the story of sex abuse in the Catholic Church is a very important narrative that mandates a candid and honest treatment. Unfortunately, as this book demonstrates, the *Globe* fell woefully short in providing such an analysis.

NOTES

[1] The investigative staff of The Boston Globe. *Betrayal: The crisis in the Catholic Church* (paperback ed.). Boston: Little, Brown and Company, 2003, p. 32.

1

A Horror Ignored

Harbor Middle School is barely over a mile away from the headquarters of the *Boston Globe*, and what occurred there on Monday, December 12, 2011, can only be described as a nightmare for any parent, student, and educator. It was on that day that a teacher – by pure accident – walked into a room to find a Special Education assistant, 37-year-old La Shawn Hill, in the act of sexually assaulting a completely defenseless, non-verbal, autistic, 14-year-old boy.

Shortly after the stomach-turning attack, the mother of the helpless child was still trying to determine the breadth of what had occurred. After being told that her son was either raped or molested by the very person entrusted to protect him, the mother reported, "All I know is that my son [will] have to go through the whole STD thing, take HIV medicine for the next 28 days, and go through the whole mental emotional trauma."[1]

But the story does not end here. It turns out that this very assistant had attacked at least one other child before at another school. Nine months earlier, the principal of Martin

Luther King, Jr. School, Jessica Bolt, became aware that Hill may have sexually assaulted an innocent 7-year-old boy. Yet Hill never alerted the police or notified the state, as clearly required by law. It later turned out that the attack was tragically true.[2]

And what did Boston Public Schools do when it found out that a principal's inaction led to the brutal sexual assault of a second tender child? The district simply administered a minor two-week suspension against the principal Hill, and then it quietly returned her back to her job.[3]

In other words, here was a case of sex abuse and cover-up almost exactly like those over which the *Globe* went apoplectic when it came to the Catholic Church decades earlier. Yet when it came to this shocking *present-day* episode, the *Globe* had very little to say at all.

The paper printed a couple of pedestrian news articles about the story, and the most that the *Globe* editorial board could muster to say about the episode was that there was a "notable misjudgment" by the principal Bolt when she failed to report a suspected child molester of special needs students to police.[4] *Globe* writers like Michael Rezendes, Walter V. Robinson, Eileen McNamara, Derrick Z. Jackson, Kevin Cullen, and Joan Vennochi – all of whom barely left a stone unturned when frenetically lambasting the Catholic Church for its handling of abuse cases from decades earlier – went completely mute when it came to this stomach-turning case right down the street from their own cubicles. There was not a syllable of criticism from any of them this time around.

A similar silence followed another episode just a few months later. In a profile article about Boston Public Schools superintendent Carol Johnson, the *Globe* buried the fact that Johnson had recently fired a teacher "accused of inappropriate contact with students" and was "in the process of finding a new position" for the principal who worked at the same school.

Boston Public Schools refused to release the name of the teacher who was being fired and would not disclose the reason why it was moving the school's principal, citing "protected personnel information."[5]

Yet the *Globe* did not rush to a courthouse to demand the very same personnel information it had ordered just a decade earlier from the Catholic Church. Nor did the paper feel the need to unleash its so-called "Spotlight Team" to investigate the scope of horrific sex abuse and callous cover-ups occurring right down the street from its offices.

Instead, around the very same time as these episodes, the *Globe* found the time and space to trumpet not one but *two* front-page stories about alleged abuse committed decades earlier by a Catholic priest – in Chicago.[6]

The double standard could not be more glaring.

NOTES

1 "Mother Says Autistic Son May Have Been Sexually Assaulted At Dorchester School," CBS Boston, December 12, 2011.

2 "Prosecutors Bring New Charges Against Former Teacher's Assistant," Suffolk County District Attorney, May 4, 2012.

3 Bolt quietly retired with full benefits in April 2013.

4 "Sex-abuse case in Boston school exposes a lack of vigilance" (editorial), *The Boston Globe*, Dec 19, 2011, p. A14.

5 James Vaznis, "School chief plans review of top staff," *The Boston Globe*, July 21, 2012, p. A1.

6 "Boston Globe Little Concerned With Child Abuse – Unless It's In the Catholic Church," TheMediaReport.com, April 16, 2002.

2

A Textbook Double Standard

> "During my schoolboy days in Aspen [in the 1970s], it was widely known that at least six teachers had sex with high school and middle school students, resulting in at least two pregnancies. Nobody went to jail, was fired or was even reprimanded."
> – Roger Marolt, Snowmass Village, Colorado[1]

When the *Globe* and its crack "Spotlight Team" ignored the atrocious abuse and cover-ups in Boston's public schools, it was not as if the paper could plead ignorance to the documented reports about such abuse and cover-ups in schools across the United States.

In 1998, *Education Week* – "American education's newspaper of record" – published an eye-popping, three-week study on educator misconduct in America's public schools. One of its articles chronicled the astonishing practice of "passing the trash," in which sexually abusive teachers – often called "mobile molesters" – go from one school to another completely unscathed.

The paper stunningly reported that it was "no secret" that schools have routinely shuffled known child molesters around to different schools and cut secret deals in doing so. School administrators do not just keep quiet, reported *Education Week*, but "they sing the employees' praises in letters of reference designed to help [the abusive teachers] move on."[2]

Meanwhile, a few years later, in 2004, the United States Department of Education released a stunning report by Hofstra University's Charol Shakeshaft. Harmonizing a number of large-sample studies of our nation's public schools, Shakeshaft concluded that "more than 4.5 million students are subject to sexual misconduct by an employee of a school sometime between kindergarten and 12th grade." Shakeshaft also added, "[A 2003 report] that nearly 9.6 percent of students are targets of educator sexual misconduct sometime during their school career presents the most accurate data available at this time."[3]

Amazingly, Shakeshaft also added that she believes that studies of the issue actually *"under-estimate"* the extent of this sickening problem.

Then, in October 2007, the Associated Press published a stunning three-part series on child sex abuse in public schools. After seven months of research it "found 2,570 educators whose teaching credentials were revoked, denied, surrendered or sanctioned from 2001 through 2005 following allegations of sexual misconduct." Just like the *Education Week* study eight years earlier, the series documented the widespread practice of "passing the trash" and the commonality of the "mobile molester."[4]

Also included in the AP series was the sickening case of a

teacher who kidnapped "more than 20 girls, some as young as 9. Among other things, he told prosecutors that he put rags in the girls' mouths, taped them shut and also bound their hands and feet with duct tape and rope for his own sexual stimulation."[5]

What about schools calling the police to report abuse by teachers? It wasn't even on the radar.

In that 2004 government report, Dr. Shakeshaft cited a 1994 study of 225 cases of educator sexual abuse in New York, in which "all of the accused had admitted to sexual abuse of a student but none of the abusers was reported to authorities."

Here is another look at that alarming fact:

Number of abusive educators: 225
Number reported to police: 0

So, in other words, as recently as 1994, it was the *universal* practice in New York among school administrators not to call police to report child molesters.

Yet the *Globe* and its Spotlight Team have never found the sickening abuse of children in public schools anything to explore in depth.

NOTES

1 Roger Marolt, "Catholic Church bigger than its crimes" (letter), *Aspen Times*, September 29, 2014.
2 Caroline Hendrie, "'Passing the Trash' by School Districts Frees Sexual Predators To Hunt Again," *Education Week*, December 9, 1998.
3 Charol Shakeshaft, "Educator Sexual Misconduct: A Synthesis of

Existing Literature," U.S. Department of Education, 2004.

4 Martha Irvine and Robert Tanner, "Sexual Misconduct Plagues US Schools," Associated Press, October 21, 2007. (Archived at washingtonpost.com)

5 Martha Irvine, "Teacher Sex Abuse Scars Family, Town," Associated Press, October 22, 2007. (Archived at washingtonpost.com)

3

Ask Beth?

Beginning in 1963, Thomas Winship, the editor of the *Boston Globe*, asked his wife, Radcliffe graduate Elizabeth Coolidge Winship, to author an advice column aimed at the paper's teenage readers. The resulting column evolved into a regular feature called "Ask Beth," in which Winship answered very candidly to her teen readers' frank questions about sexual behavior, puberty, masturbation, relationships, and homosexuality.

No topic appeared too "hot" or off-limits for "Ask Beth." *Globe* readers frequently encountered some real eye-opening letters with their morning coffee if they stumbled upon Winship's column over breakfast. (For example, August 7, 1980: "Dear Beth: I am 15 and my penis is very small …")

On June 17, 1980, the *Globe* published an especially astonishing "Ask Beth" letter from a high school boy who said he had impregnated his 31-year-old teacher after she seduced him. (Read the actual letter on page 15.)

Unquestionably, a crime had been committed, but readers

never would have known it from Winship and the *Globe*. In replying to the victim, Winship said nothing to the boy about the fact that the teacher had committed a serious sex crime and that he should immediately report the teacher to the police and the school.

Rather, Winship actually chastised the boy for "not resisting," as if the boy bore fault!

Meanwhile, the headline to the column carried the headline, "An encounter with a teacher," as if pregnancy-inducing sex between these two was merely an "encounter."[1]

Also, most notably, there was not a syllable of follow-up from the *Globe* whatsoever about this shocking case. Not a single writer at the *Globe* thought it was newsworthy to further pursue the story of a local teacher sexually abusing a student and then becoming pregnant. The crack Spotlight Team apparently was not very outraged at the criminal betrayal that had taken place.

And Winship's warped advice was hardly an isolated episode. Only three days after publishing the student-teacher-pregnancy story, the *Globe* published a letter from a different teen – this one a girl with a crush on her science teacher. "I dream of him every night," she wrote. "Is it OK to write to him?"

Winship's response: "Send him one postcard. A heavy correspondence would only build false hopes, but you can't get too intimate on a card."[2]

"Hopes"? Hopes of *what*? And Winship made no mention that any "intimacy" between a student and her teacher would not just be inappropriate, but criminal.

During its coverage of the Catholic Church abuse

scandals, *Globe* columnists frequently castigated Church officials for failing to call the police decades ago when confronted with suspicions that priests had abused minors.

Yet notifying the police was never even the advice of the *Globe's own columnists* when it came to child sex crimes by adults. Go figure.

An "encounter with a teacher" or a *crime*?

An encounter with a teacher

Dear Beth:

I'm a male senior, 17, tall, and considered good-looking. One of my teachers is 31, beautiful, and married. She asked me to stay after class and then seduced me. I must say I didn't resist. I assumed she was on the Pill, but she has just informed me she's pregnant, and as she's having marital problems, I must be the father.

What should I do? I think I love her, and want to keep the baby, but she asked me to pay for an abortion.

— D.S.

June 17, 1980: Readers of the Globe *never would have known a crime was committed when a high-school boy reported being sexually abused by his teacher.*

NOTES

[1] Ask Beth, “An encounter with a teacher,” *The Boston Globe*, June 17, 1980.
[2] Ask Beth, “Alternatives to spanking,” *The Boston Globe*, June 20, 1980.

4

Touting Incest Supporters at the *Globe*

Elizabeth Winship's shocking "Ask Beth" advice in the *Boston Globe* was not just limited to downplaying child sex crimes between teachers and students.

In several columns over the years, Winship answered questions from readers about which books she recommended for sex education for youngsters. One book which Winship repeatedly recommended to her impressionable young readers was *Girls and Sex* by Wardell B. Pomeroy,[1] who was an internationally renowned "sexologist" and research partner of the notorious Alfred Kinsey.

To say that some of Pomeroy's views on sexuality were eye-opening is an understatement. Pomeroy actually once opined that sex between adults and children "can sometimes be beneficial."[2] Pomeroy even wrote positively of incest, of the virtues of sex between fathers and daughters. According to Pomeroy:

> "We find many beautiful and mutually satisfying [sexual] relationships between fathers and daughters. These may

> be transient or ongoing, but they have no harmful effects … Incest between adults and younger children can also prove to be a satisfying and enriching experience …
> "When there is a mutual and unselfish concern for the other person, rather than a feeling of possessiveness and a selfish concern with one's own sexual gratification, then incestuous relationships can and do work out well. Incest can be a satisfying, non-threatening, and even an enriching emotional experience."[3]

That's right. The *Globe* openly and repeatedly promoted an author who celebrated sex between fathers and daughters and added that it was "enriching" and "satisfying."

As far as Pomeroy's *Girls and Sex* – which the *Globe*'s Winship enthusiastically recommended numerous times – the book is completely uninhibited in its language and its approach to topics such as masturbation, homosexuality, and sexual practices.

Some of Pomeroy's passages are just plain disturbing, if not outright stomach-turning. In a chapter about some of the "early sexual experiences" that a young girl may have, Pomeroy writes:

- *"Sometimes men (mostly strangers) expose their penises to a young girl because of mental problems … Men like this are almost never dangerous"* (page 49).

"Never dangerous"? Pomeroy also says nothing about this perverted deed actually being a *crime* and that a girl or her family should immediately call the police.

- *"Another not uncommon experience occurs when a girl goes alone to the cinema and a man sitting beside her slips a hand under her thigh or otherwise makes some kind of sexual advance. The remedy is a simple one. Simply get up and move to another seat. If he persists, call the usherette"* (page 49).

That's right. If a grown male molests a young girl in a movie theater, Pomeroy's advice is for the child to merely move her seat or simply notify the "usherette" (who is probably just some teenager working at the theater part-time). Again, Pomeroy says absolutely nothing about a sex crime having been committed and police being notified.

- *"It has always been a natural part of a child's development to look at and explore the bodies of other young children, to examine the similarities and differences, and to get some sexual pleasure from doing it. Mistakenly, parents forbid this harmless sexual activity"* (page 44).

It has "always" been "natural" and "harmless" for children to sexually molest each other and "get some sexual pleasure" from doing so? Really?

In a different chapter in *Girls and Sex* about dating, Pomeroy opines about a theoretical 14-year-old girl "going out with the thirty-five-year-old father of the child for whom she baby sits" (page 61).

14-year-old girl. 35-year-old father. Got it?

What does Pomeroy think of such an arrangement?

"It is possible that even this relationship could be a positive one, but the odds are so heavily against its turning out to be anything but disastrous."

Pomeroy also adds that it would be "sheer agony" for the grown man to even contemplate divorcing his wife and running off with the girl.

Notice that Pomeroy says absolutely nothing about such a scenario being a serious crime and being totally inappropriate. Pomeroy believes the hypothetical episode is "disastrous" not because a grown adult is using his power and taking sexual advantage of a young teenager and abusing her, but only because "the odds are so heavily against" the relationship actually succeeding.

> "If she is willing to put up with empty weekends, surreptitious meetings, and be content with having only a part of a man, then she is entitled to whatever short-changed satisfaction she can get, I suppose" (page 62).

In other words, Pomeroy is hardly condemning of a "relationship" between a 14-year-old girl and a 35-year-old married man. Unbelievable.

Beth Winship enthusiastically recommended this perverted book no less than ***ten*** times in the pages of the *Boston Globe* over the years to her readers,[4] once actually advising it to girls as young as *12.*[5]

Mitigating child sex abuse with support from the *Globe*

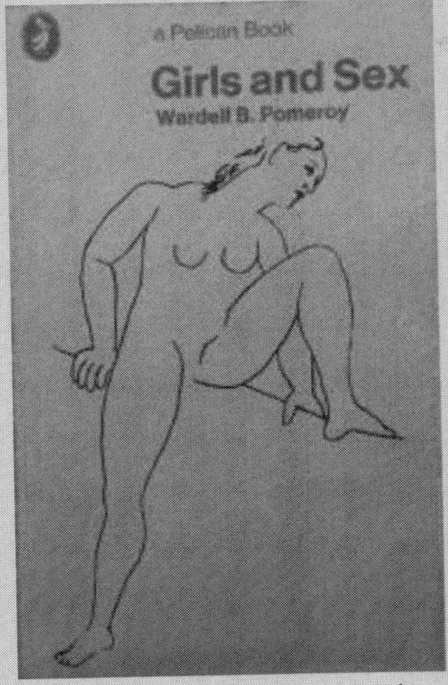

The cover of Wardell Pomeroy's shocking and disturbing Girls and Sex, *which the* Boston Globe *enthusiastically and repeatedly recommended to its child readers.*

NOTES

1 Wardell B. Pomeroy (1971). *Girls and sex.* England: Penguin Books.

2 "Attacking the Last Taboo: Researchers are lobbying against the

ban on incest," *Time*, April 14, 1980, p. 72.

[3] Wardell B. Pomeroy, "A New Look at Incest," *Variations* (magazine), January 1977, pages 86 to 88; and *Forum* (magazine), November 1976, pages 84 to 89.

[4] The ten instances are in *Boston Globe* columns on March 31, 1977; May 1, 1977; October 5, 1978; August 12, 1979; September 2, 1980; November 9, 1980; November 5, 1981; April 4, 1982; May 9, 1982; and February 17, 1983.

[5] Ask Beth, "Books about sex," *The Boston Globe*, May 9, 1982, p.SM56.

5

A-OK at *The Boston Globe*

By the mid-1970s, film director Roman Polanski was one of Hollywood's most celebrated figures. Tinseltown showered numerous accolades and awards upon him for his directorial prowess for such movies as *Rosemary's Baby* and *Chinatown*, two of his most notable works.

Yet on Thursday afternoon, March 10, 1977, Roman Polanski picked up 13-year-old Samantha Gailey from her home and drove her to the residence of his friend, Jack Nicholson, under the auspices of taking photographs of the young girl for a Paris *Vogue* magazine photo layout.

At the Nicholson house, Polanski plied the underage Samantha with champagne and took pictures of her holding her half-empty champagne glass. He then furnished to her a quaalude pill, a very powerful tranquilizer.

Then, while Samantha was in a drugged and weakened state, and despite her numerous efforts to resist him, Polanski removed the girl's underwear. He then performed oral sex on his underage victim. Also against her will, he then raped her vaginally and then sodomized her.

After his brutal attack, Polanski drove Samantha back to her home during which Polanski told Samantha that his attack would be "our secret."

"You know," Polanski confided to Samantha in the car, "when I first met you, I promised myself that I wouldn't do anything like this with you." Samantha was still wearing her soiled underwear.[1]

Now if the brutal drugging and sadistic rape of a 13-year-old girl upset anyone at the *Boston Globe*, it surely did not let any of its readers know about it. In fact, after the attack the paper showered not only effusive praise upon the criminal director but also outright sympathy.

Within months after Polanski's savage attack, the *Globe* was already merely referring to his crimes as a "morals conviction"[2] and a "sex case,"[3] while one column joked that Polanski's next film would be entitled, *Close Encounters With the Third Grade*, a perverted twist on the title of a popular science-fiction movie at the time.[4] Hilarious.

In 1979, only a year after Polanski fled the United States to France to avoid punishment for his sex crimes, one of the *Globe*'s film critics, Bruce McCabe, joined Polanski at the famed Cannes Film Festival in promotion of the filmmaker's new film, *Tess*. A press conference at the festival became quite raucous as journalists from a fevered media peppered Polanski with questions about his rape and his escape from justice.

In a column about the press conference, McCabe lamented, "I've never heard anyone, public or private, subjected to such abuse." Yet there was not a syllable from McCabe about the abuse that Polanski's rape victim undoubtedly suffered.[5]

And when McCabe got around to publishing a review of Polanski's *Tess* in 1981, the rape of Samantha Gailey was already a distant memory. McCabe made no mention of the filmmaker's crimes at all. He did note, however, that *Tess* was "truly awesome" and "one of those rare treasures that restores one's faith in the efficacy of the cinema."[6]

Another *Globe* film critic, Michael Blowen, was equally effusive of Polanski. Blowen beamed that *Tess* was "simply awesome" and "ranks among the most spiritually compelling films of our time."

And as for Polanski himself? Well, Blowen raved that the child rapist was a "classic romantic." He also bemoaned the fact that ever since his trial "Polanski has been depicted as an insensitive, child molestor [*sic*],"[7] as if readers were somehow supposed to think something different.

But the *Globe*'s Blowen saved his best for Polanski a year later, in 1981, with a glowing 1,400-word profile of the famed director, which also featured an interview.

In Blowen's piece, the rape of the 13-year-old Gailey was downgraded to merely one of "life's vicissitudes." (A "vicissitude" is defined as "a change of circumstances or fortune, typically unwelcome or unpleasant.") And Polanski was hardly apologetic about his criminal attack from only a few years earlier. In fact, Polanski *defended* his crimes:

> "I can't get specific, but let me say this – there are 13-year-old girls who look and act like they're 10, and there are 13-year-old girls who look and act like they're 25. She acted old enough …
>
> "I was taking photographs and one thing led to another … European authorities would never prosecute a case like that. It's much better for me here [in Paris]."[8]

Neither Blowen nor anyone at the *Globe* was outraged at Polanski's defense. Neither were there any nasty editorials from the paper castigating Polanski. Maybe it was because a few years earlier, the *Globe* had published a column that matter-of-factly informed its readers that it was a common practice in Hollywood for film studios to "buy off" and "take care" of celebrities who "got in trouble" with underage sex crimes.

According to the article, Hollywood studio bosses would "contribute generously to the campaigns of local district attorneys," who, in turn, would "'take care' of studio stars who got in trouble."[9] Interesting.

Yet the *Globe*'s "Spotlight Team" declined to further examine this shocking practice.

Just one of those misfortunes in life?

Polanski riding out life's vicissitudes

'I do the best I can with what life's given me'

This Boston Globe *headline shows that by 1981, the paper had already reduced the drugging, sex assault, and forced sodomy of a 13-year-old by Hollywood director Roman Polanski to merely one of "life's vicissitudes." (Headline from February 15, 1981.)*

NOTES

1 All of the details from Polanski's crime are taken from the deposition given by the victim Samantha Gailey during grand jury proceedings in Los Angeles on Thursday, March 24, 1977.

2 "Polanski Staying in Paris," *The Boston Globe*, February 11, 1978, p. 15.

3 "Trial judge wanted Polanski out of U.S.," *The Boston Globe*, February 7, 1978, p. 2.

4 Walter Scott, "Personality Parade," *The Boston Globe*, January 29, 1978, p. K2.

5 Bruce McCabe, "Just your average day at Cannes," *The Boston Globe*, May 20, 1979, p. A10.

6 Bruce McCabe, "Polanski creates an exquisite *Tess*," *The Boston Globe*, Feb 13, 1981.

7 Michael Blowen, "Tess of D'Ubervilles' beautiful work from a tarnished filmmaker," *The Boston Globe*, Dec. 26, 1980.

8 Michael Blowen, "Polanski riding out life's vicissitudes; 'I do the best I can with what life's given me'," *The Boston Globe*, February 15, 1981.

9 Walter Scott, "Personality Parade," *The Boston Globe*, June 5, 1977.

6

The *Globe* Endorses an Abuser for U.S. Congress

In 1972, the people of Massachusetts' 12th district, in Southeastern Massachusetts, elected Gerry E. Studds to the United States House of Representatives. Within a short time, Studds developed a strong reputation for representing his area's fishing industry, which was vital to his region's economic health.

However, the Democratic politician harbored some personal secrets, and 11 years later, in 1983, these secrets exploded into the public arena.

On July 20, 1983, by a vote of 421-3, Congress censured Studds for having sexual relations with a Congressional school-aged male page and making sexual advances to two others.[1] In the spring and summer of 1973, Studds regularly took a young page back to his tony Georgetown apartment, where he often plied the youngster with vodka-cranberry drinks and had sex with him. He also took the page on a lavish two-and-a-half week trip to Europe, where the booze continued to flow and the sex persisted.[2]

The relationship was obviously a gross abuse of power.

When Congress first announced that it would reprimand Studds for his conduct, the Congressman arranged a media event to address the issue, and Studds read from a prepared statement. Shockingly, the first words from Studds had nothing to do with apologizing for his misdeeds or recognizing the exploitation of power that had taken place.

Studds' first words were bemoaning "the challenge of initiating and maintaining a career in public office without destroying entirely the ability to lead a meaningful and emotionally fulfilling private life."

Then two sentences later, Studds let out a whopper: "[T]hese challenges are made substantially more complex when one is, as am I, both an elected public official and gay."[3]

Boom. And with that, the *Boston Globe* and the rest of the media fell over themselves to celebrate the country's "first openly gay member of Congress."

From a public relations standpoint, Studds' maneuver was a stroke of genius. Studds successfully steered the episode away from being about a Congressman using his position of power to sexually abuse a young page to being about a man "courageously" acknowledging in public that he was gay. By doing so, Studds not only averted a p.r. catastrophe but created a sympathetic portrait for himself. And the *Boston Globe* gladly embraced such a depiction.

A political adversary of Studds would later observe, "If you talk to the people in [his] district, they don't realize the age of the boy, they don't realize that liquor was involved, they don't realize that this same boy was the boy that was taken to Europe with the congressman … The congressman has done a grand job of making this appear as a homosexual issue."[4]

Within days of Studds' historic announcement, the *Globe* was relaying supporters' beliefs that Studds' revelation was "dignified" and "historic."[5] The paper also turned to Democratic supporters who heralded that Studds was a "first-rate member of Congress" and "one hell of a congressman" who is "articulate, concerned and compassionate."[6]

Lost in the *Globe* coverage was that Studds never actually apologized for his abusive conduct and only admitted to an "error in judgment." In truth, Studds actually *disagreed* with Congress' conclusion that his egregious behavior constituted "improper sexual conduct," claiming that the sex with the page was "mutual and voluntary" and part of a "private, consensual relationship."[7]

And unlike years later when the paper was wagging its finger at the Catholic Church for the abuse of teenage boys, no one at the *Globe* demanded that Studds be removed from public office or undergo a psychological examination. No one at the *Globe* breathlessly asked why the police were never notified of a possible crime.

Instead, when Gerry Studds was up for re-election a year later in 1984 in his district, the *Globe* took its ultimate stand on the issue of a powerful Congressman plying a high-school boy with booze, having sex repeatedly with him, and taking him on an outing to Europe (with more booze and sex).

The *Globe* heartily endorsed Studds for re-election. "Studds in the tenth" was the paper's proud headline in an editorial on October 26, 1984, with Studds' glaring abuse of a young page being reduced to merely a "moral transgression."[8]

A ringing endorsement from the *Globe*

Studds in the Tenth

The Boston Globe endorses Gerry E. Studds for re-election to the US House of Representa- **pages. It w** **Yet the**

Even though Massachusetts Congressman Gerry Studds admitted to repeatedly having sex with a high-school-aged boy and plying him with booze (in addition to taking him on a trip to Europe), that did not stop the Globe *from showering Studds with an important re-election endorsement on October 26, 1984.*

NOTES

[1] "House Censures Studds, Crane," *The Boston Globe*, July 21, 1983.
[2] "Report of the Committee on Standards of Official Conduct on the Inquiry Under House Resolution 12, 98th Congress, 1st Session," July 14, 1983.
[3] "Statement by Studds," *The Boston Globe*, July 15, 1983.
[4] David Farrell, "Turning point in Studds-Flynn race?" *The Boston Globe*, July 2, 1984.
[5] David Rogers, "The page scandal and Congress' image," *The Boston Globe*, July 17, 1983.
[6] Susan Trausch, "Studds tells the House of error," *The Boston Globe*, July 15, 1983.
[7] "Statement by Studds."
[8] "Studds in the tenth" (editorial), *The Boston Globe*, October 26, 1984. Because of redistricting that took place in Massachusetts in 1981 or '82, Studds went from representing the Twelfth District to the Tenth.

7

Pelted With Condoms? "Peaceful"?

The ordination of a man to the priesthood is supposed to be an incredibly joyous day, not just for the priest himself but for his family as well.

However, such was not the case on Saturday, June 16, 1990, at Holy Cross Cathedral in Boston, when Cardinal Bernard Law and the Archdiocese of Boston welcomed 11 men to the priesthood.

Two gay activist groups and an abortion lobbying group[1] led hundreds of loud and angry demonstrators outside the cathedral to stage a "protest" against Cardinal Law and the Church's teachings on abortion and sexuality. What transpired at the event can only be described as breathtaking.

The details of what occurred at the demonstration have never been in dispute. Indeed, protestors outside the ordination:

- threw condoms at priests and their families as they exited the cathedral;[2] [3]
- hurled obscenities and chants at priests and their families;[4] [5]

- attempted to disrupt the Mass inside by blowing whistles and sounding air horns from the sidewalk;[6]
- shouted "Shame, shame, shame" and "Come out of the closet" as they followed the newly ordained priests and their families to their cars;[7]
- defaced a sidewalk with obscenity;[8]
- ridiculed the Eucharist by placing condoms between Communion wafers;[9] and
- staged a mockery of the Mass featuring women dressed as men, vulgarity, and simulated sex acts.[10]

Yet how did the *Boston Globe*, the area's paper of record, cover this horrendous affront to Catholics and the attack on clergy that day? Here is the opening sentence of the *Globe*'s coverage the next day after the ordination:

> "Hundreds of advocates for homosexuals' rights, AIDS education and abortion rights staged a colorful, loud – and peaceful – demonstration yesterday outside Holy Cross Cathedral to protest the political stances of Cardinal Bernard Law."[11]

"Peaceful"?? One cannot help but wonder if the *Globe* would have chosen such a benign description to depict a protest targeting those of another religious faith. Would the *Globe* have chosen the word "peaceful" to describe a group of cursing anti-Semites hurling condoms and slurs at rabbis outside a temple while ridiculing their faith?

Would the *Globe* have chosen the word "peaceful" to describe a group of cursing homophobes hurling condoms and epithets at gay men outside a gay nightclub? No way.

With any other religion or group, the *Globe* would have

been screaming "hate crimes." Yet to the *Globe*, the bigoted attacks at a Catholic ordination ceremony were simply "colorful, loud, and peaceful." Unreal.

And quite ironically, on the very same day that demonstrators were disrupting an ordination with the claim that the Church was doing "nothing" to care for those with AIDS, just down the road in Hartford, Connecticut, the Vatican's president for the Pontifical Council for Pastoral Assistance to Health Care Workers was visiting a residence operated by the Church especially for people suffering with AIDS. He also addressed reporters about proposals to further strengthen the Church's response to the AIDS crisis.[12]

The *Globe*, however, did not report a single syllable about this notable story.

"Peaceful"?

As police used barricades to hold back the mob, gay activists and protesters tossed condoms, ridiculed Catholicism, and hurled obscenities at newly ordained priests and their families in Boston, on June 16, 1990. Yet the next day, the Globe *actually characterized the episode as "peaceful." (Photo: BCTV)*

NOTES

[1] The three groups were ACT-UP (AIDS Coalition To Unleash Power), the Massachusetts Coalition for Lesbian and Gay Civil Rights, and the Reproductive Right Network.
[2] Jack Meyers and Gary Witherspoon, "Protesters rip church for AIDS, abort stand," *The Boston Herald*, June 17, 1990, p. 5. (Also, "Christian-bashing" (letter), *The Pilot*, June 29, 1990, p. 16.)
[3] "Stark Contrast" (editorial), *The Pilot*, June 22, 1990, p. 12.
[4] Meyers and Witherspoon.
[5] "Stark Contrast."
[6] Meyers and Witherspoon.
[7] Meyers and Witherspoon.
[8] "Stark Contrast" (with photo showing the sidewalk)
[9] Ibid.
[10] "Christian-bashing"
[11] Irene Sege, "Hundreds protest Cardinal Law at ordination," *The Boston Globe*, June 17, 1990.
[12] Fr. Bill Pomerleau, "Vatican may sponsor regional meetings for people with AIDS," *The Pilot* (Catholic News Service), June 22, 1990, p. 8.

8

Bring on the Psychologists

"No one would hold a brain surgeon to today's standard of care for professional decisions he made in 1970. Yet the decisions made in 1970 by Catholic bishops, who routinely consulted with mental health professionals about sick priests, are being judged by today's standards. Today, the confidence of the mental health community about the likelihood of curing sexual disorders is far less than it was in 1970." – L. Martin Nussbaum[1]

"On countless occasions, psychologists gave bishops terrible advice about abusive priests – and, of course, this bad advice led to terrible consequences for victims and the broader church. Yet these psychologists have gotten off scot-free in the media."
– U.S. District Court Judge Patrick J. Schiltz[2]

There is a lot more to the case of filmmaker Roman Polanski (from Chapter 5), and the Polanski episode helps to illustrate the most underreported aspect of the Catholic Church abuse story as reported by the *Boston Globe* and the rest of the mainstream media.

In the weeks after Polanski's arrest in March 1977, a

judge ordered the director to a 90-day psychiatric evaluation at California's Chino State Prison, where he was visited by a number of professional psychologists.

After a mere 42 days, Polanski's evaluation was completed, and the director was released from custody. A state probation officer completed and issued a 29-page report based on the conclusions that the team of psychologists had reached. By today's standards, the contents of the report are nothing less than stunning.

"Jail is not being recommended at the present time," the report stated matter-of-factly. "The present offense appears to have been spontaneous and an exercise of poor judgement [*sic*] by the defendant."

The report also quoted psychologist Dr. Alvin E. Davis, who had evaluated Polanski and wrote, "[Polanski] is not mentally ill or disordered ... He is of superior intelligence, has good judgement and strong moral and ethical values, and has normal remorse for his offense ..."

Shockingly, Dr. Davis also cited the "physical maturity and willingness and provocativeness of [the] victim" as a mitigating factor to Polanski's guilt.

In other words, Davis believed that the 13-year-old victim herself somehow contributed to her own rape.

The probation officer's report also cited numerous other reasons why Polanski should not be harshly punished for his crimes, including:

- "Incarceration would serve no necessary or useful purpose but would impose an unusual degree of stress and hardship because of his highly sensitive personality and devotion to his work";
- "He is especially fearful of interference with his occupation"; and

- "[The crime] was neither an aggressive nor forceful sexual act."

Again, here is a summary of Polanski's crime: He plied a 13-year-old girl with champagne. He then dispensed a quaalude tranquilizer to her. He then – against the girl's will – performed oral sex, vaginal intercourse, and sodomy upon the girl.

And a psychologist concluded that Polanski was of "good judgement [*sic*]."

In truth, the Polanski case illustrates perfectly how psychologists – as well as society as a whole – treated the abuse of minors in the 1970s. To tragic results, the abuse of minors was far-too-often viewed as a psychological "illness" that could be attended to with "treatment." Today we know much better.

As psychologist Monica Applewhite has explained:

> "From the 1950's to the 1980's, [] treatment-based interventions for sexual criminals were not only enormously prevalent in the United States, but surveys of ordinary citizens showed that they were enormously popular …
>
> "[T]he science of human sexuality and sexual offending is extraordinarily young. Virtually all of the information we utilize today regarding the treatment and supervision of sexual offenders has been discovered since 1985."[3]

Yet in the volumes and volumes of the *Boston Globe*'s coverage of Catholic clergy sex abuse in 2002, this reality was barely addressed. When the Church was sending accused priests to psychological treatment, even "the criminal justice system was doing the very same thing with convicted offenders – sending them to treatment instead of prison."[4]

Indeed, even with the tragic case of John Geoghan, each and every parish assignment following his first complaint of sex abuse was only after "an independent medical evaluation advising that such assignment was appropriate and safe."[5]

And if anyone during the *Globe*'s 2002 coverage wanted to learn the truth about the way society and psychologists used to deal with child sex abuse, they could look to the paper's *very own reporting* only a decade earlier …

NOTES

[1] L. Martin Nussbaum, "Changing the Rules," *America* (magazine), May 15, 2006.

[2] Patrick J. Schiltz, "Not all the news is fit to print: What the media missed in the sexual-abuse scandal," *Commonweal*, August 15, 2003.

[3] "Address of Dr. Monica Applewhite to the Irish Bishops," March 10, 2009. Available at http://www.themediareport.com/wp-content/uploads/2012/11/Applewhite-Ireland-Address-Bishops-2009.pdf

[4] Tim Drake, "'Change in Vatican Culture': A Sex Abuse Expert Sees Hope in Pope Benedict," National Catholic Register, April 16, 2010.

[5] Wilson D. Rogers, Jr., "A letter to the editor of *The Pilot*," *The Pilot*, July 27, 2001, pp. 1, 5.

9

Ten Years Earlier …

When the *Boston Globe* excoriated the Archdiocese of Boston in 2002 for relying on therapists to treat abusive priests from the 1950s to the 1990s, the paper somehow apparently forgot that in 1992 the *Globe* itself was enthusiastically trumpeting the psychological treatment of sex offenders as "highly effective" and "dramatic."

A front-page article in the *Globe* on June 18, 1992, began as follows:

> "A new generation of treatment programs for sex offenders is proving highly effective, dramatically reducing the percentage of cases in which offenders repeat sex crimes, research shows.
>
> "Recidivism rates declined from 9 percent for untreated offenders to 5 percent for those who underwent the new treatment in one study, and from 38 percent to 6 percent in another.
>
> "While there is no complete 'cure' for sex offenders, the

> new findings indicate that many of them can learn to manage their aberrant sexual impulses without committing new crimes. The promising new treatments focus on helping these offenders control the complex cauldron of social inadequacies, distorted thinking, and deviant sex fantasies that prompt them to rape women, molest children or exhibit themselves in public."[1]

Indeed, the *Globe* editorial board itself was also an ardent proponent of therapeutic treatment for sex offenders. In an editorial only eight days after the above article, the *Globe* editorial board published "An offender's right to treatment," which forcefully petitioned the Governor of Massachusetts at the time (William Weld) for "improved treatment programs" in the state, contending that it was "wrong to impose harsh punishments on sexually violent criminals without offering them treatment."[2]

Around the same time, the *Globe* also published another article seemingly endorsing the manner in which the Catholic Church handled abusive priests. Under the headline, "Ways cited to treat those who abuse," the *Globe* wrote:

> "[Those who treat sex offenders] and other specialists said many offenders can be returned to active ministry so long as the clergy and their supervisors accept lifelong restrictions and follow-up care."[3]

The *Globe* went on to say that "society will suffer" if offenders are not afforded therapeutic treatment, as such measures are "cost-effective" and successful.

The hypocrisy here is rich. After first promoting psychological treatment for sex offenders in 1992 – including the Church's own treatment programs for offending priests –

by 2002 the *Globe* was scolding the Church for doing in 1992 exactly what the *Globe* itself said it should be doing!

Certainly, if the *Globe* had questioned or challenged the wisdom of such treatments for priests and other members of society at the time, it could have unleashed its crack Spotlight Team to delve deeper into the issue. But it didn't.

Instead, the *Globe* waited ten years after memories of these heralded treatments had faded and general society's approach to such measures had changed dramatically.

Ways cited to treat priests who abuse

By James L. Franklin
GLOBE STAFF

This July 1992 article is proof that the Boston Globe *already knew many years before 2002 that the Church was attempting to treat abusive priests with therapy treatments and return them to active ministry.*

New therapy seen to cut repeat sex crimes

By Alison Bass
GLOBE STAFF

went the new treatment in one study, and from 38 percent to 6 ...

equacies, distorted thinking, and deviant sex fantasies that prompt ...

An offender's right to treatment. . .

In 1992, the Globe *was already regularly trumpeting the issue of sex abuse by priests in the Catholic Church. And with nary a syllable of criticism, it was also heralding "highly effective" and "dramatic" therapy treatment of sex offenders that allowed them to be released to the public. In fact, the* Globe *editorial board openly advocated for the right of criminal sex offenders to receive such treatments. (The two headlines above are from June 1992.)*

NOTES

[1] Alison Bass, "New therapy seen to cut repeat sex crimes," *The Boston Globe*, June 18, 1992.
[2] "An offender's right to treatment" (editorial), *The Boston Globe*, June 26, 1992, p. 14.
[3] James L. Franklin, "Ways cited to treat priests who abuse," *The Boston Globe*, July 19, 1992.

10

An Outrage In Revere, But Not at the *Globe*

In December 1977, law enforcement rounded up two dozen men involved in a shocking child sex ring in Revere, a gritty city in Suffolk County just on the outskirts of Boston.

The gay sex ring reportedly involved men paying money to as many as *63* boys between the *ages of 8 and 13* over a period of at least four years.[1] The men, some of whom reportedly flew in from other areas of the country to commit their crimes, enticed their victims by offering them marijuana, beer, and cash.[2] Criminal charges against the men included rape, sodomy, "indecent assault and battery on a child under 14," and "unnatural acts with a child under 14."[3] Tragically, many of the victims were already from broken homes,[4] and some were foster children under the care of the state.[5]

About 18 months after the original arrests, a slew of the cases were finally adjudicated. On April 24, 1979, on page 21 (!), the *Boston Globe* reported that even though almost all of the men pleaded *guilty* to the various underage sex crimes, a county judge merely sentenced almost all of the defendants to *probation*. (Of the 12 cases, the one man sentenced to prison had already been determined to be a "sexually dangerous person" in a previous case.)

That's right. Grown men molested and sodomized young boys ranging in age from 8 to 13, and barely anyone saw the inside of a prison cell. How on earth did this happen? Well, the *Globe* quoted Suffolk County Assistant District Attorney Thomas Butters about the sentencing:

"First," Butters explained, "we felt under the circumstances of the cases there were no forcible sexual acts. The kids were being paid, for the most part and the activities were considered analogous to that involving a female prostitute.

"Secondly," Butters continued. "[Another judge] had set the precedent in Dr. Allen's case and I personally agreed with him."[6]

"Dr. Allen's case" involved another one of the men who was arrested in the Revere gay sex ring. Donald M. Allen, 51, was a prominent Boston psychiatrist and pediatrician, as well as a former instructor at Harvard Medical School.[7] Five months earlier, in December 1978, a jury *convicted* Allen on four counts of rape of a boy, yet a judge merely sentenced Dr. Allen to a measly five years' probation "on the condition he undergoes psychiatric treatment."[8]

How did the *Globe* react to these shockingly light sentences to men who raped and sodomized pre-teenagers? Did the *Globe* unleash its "Spotlight Team" to look into how young kids in the state's foster care system ended up as part of a homosexual child sex ring? Did the paper trumpet an editorial displaying disgust at the meager punishments doled out by the judges or the prosecutors' efforts to mitigate underage sex crimes?

Hardly. On the same day that the *Globe* published the

verdict and sentencing in the case of Dr. Allen, the paper also carried the article, "Doctor's sentence called fair." The article began:

> "Judges and trial lawyers yesterday praised Suffolk Superior Court Judge Joseph Ford for the sentence he ordered for Dr. Donald M. Allen, 51, after the doctor was convicted on statutory rape charges.
>
> "A veteran judge commented that 'the easiest sentence for a judge to impose is a severe one, but the hardest to give is one that is fair under all the circumstances to the public and the defendant.' He said Ford's sentence was 'eminently fair'."[9]

And no one at the *Globe* raised a syllable of criticism about the paltry punishments that were given.

One of the writers at the *Globe* back in 1979 was Eileen McNamara. During the *Globe*'s relentless 2002 coverage of Catholic sex abuse, McNamara would mercilessly lambaste Church officials for their handling of abuse cases back in the 1970s and 1980s.

Yet back in 1979, McNamara herself never raised a syllable of criticism for the way judges and prosecutors offered only probation for child sex crimes.

Rather, McNamara was focused on other concerns, such as theft of brass door knockers in Boston's tony Beacon Hill neighborhood.[10] Powerful stuff.

The "Spotlight Team"?

The investigation by the *Boston Globe* into Catholic Church sex abuse was a product of the paper's "Spotlight Team," a research unit that formed in 1970 and would periodically publish in-depth examinations of perceived corruption in government and other institutions.

For example, in previous years, the Spotlight Team had examined such cases as the high incidence of cancer among workers at a Navy shipyard and the Bank of Boston allegedly laundering money from organized crime.

Weeks after successfully suing the Archdiocese of Boston to obtain private personnel documents in late 2001, the *Globe* published its first article on Sunday, January 6, 2002 based on what the Spotlight Team had discovered. Under the headline splashed across the top of its front page, "Church allowed abuse by priest for years," the article was an overview of the archdiocese's handling of former priest John J. Geoghan, one of Boston's most notorious molesters.

The *Globe*, however, was just getting started. And with the Internet now in nearly every home in the industrialized world – which had not been the case only a few years earlier – the story's reach was unprecedented.

Day after day, the *Globe* relentlessly amplified the story by reporting on other troubling cases that occurred in the Archdiocese of Boston. By the time 2002 ended, the *Globe* had published an astounding **989** items about sex abuse in the Catholic Church – an average of over two-and-a-half items *per day*. The intensity with which the *Globe* pursued this story cannot be overstated.

NOTES

1 "17th arrest made in child sex probe," *The Boston Globe*, December 11, 1977, p. 58.
2 Ibid.
3 Richard Connolly, Arthur Jones, "Police say operation Revere-based," *The Boston Globe*, December 9, 1977.
4 "17th arrest."
5 Richard J. Connolly, Arthur Jones, "State to decide aid for sex-ring victims," *The Boston Globe*, December 10, 1977, p. 3.
[Joseph McCain was a veteran Boston detective who discovered the sex ring. A biographer of McCain later said about McCain's experiences with the Revere cases, "Even with all the murderers and bad guys that he put away, [McCain] would go home at night, kiss his wife, walk the dog and sleep like a baby. But when it came to these well-heeled guys, with the imprimatur of upper-crust society, secretly molesting children, it sickened him so that he could not sleep." David Mehegan, "Book him: Regular guy as crime fighter," *The New York Times*, March 18, 2005.]
6 Alan Sheehan, "12 child-sex cases decided in Suffolk," *The Boston Globe*, April 24, 1979, p. 21.
7 Nina McCain, "Impassive, calm – and controlled," *The Boston Globe*, December 17, 1978, p. 29.
8 Paul Langer, "Dr. Allen guilty, is given probation," *The Boston Globe*, December 23, 1978, p. 1.
9 Joseph Harvey, "Doctor's sentence called fair," *The Boston Globe*, December 23, 1978, p. 20.
10 Eileen McNamara, "Trouble knocking at the door," *The Boston Globe*, December 5, 1979, p. 1.

11

The *Globe* Sets the Stage For NAMBLA

In the months after the shocking arrests of several gay child molesters in Revere, the *Globe* prominently published an op-ed in April of 1978 from Boston-area resident Thomas Reeves.

Thomas Reeves was a Methodist minister and a professor of social sciences at Boston's Roxbury Community College. But, most notably, in December 1978, Reeves co-founded the notorious advocacy group NAMBLA, the North American Man/Boy Love Association, which openly advocated for the abolishment of age of consent laws and celebrated gay sex between grown men and young boys.

And the truth is that Reeves could not have been empowered to establish NAMBLA without great assistance from the *Boston Globe*.

Six months before Reeves established NAMBLA, the *Globe* gave Reeves a prominent forum in its paper to trumpet his twisted views on sex with children. Under the banner, "Fairness for all," Reeves passionately argued that the recent prosecutions of child molesters in Revere and in the Boston area had simply been part of "a witch hunt against gay people."[1]

Reeves asserted in the *Globe* that police should never have been prosecuting gay child sex crimes in the Boston area. Placing the words *child molestation* in quotation marks, Reeves claimed that there was something mitigating about the fact that the child sex acts with the young boys in Revere had supposedly been "nonviolent." (Reeves was completely oblivious to the physical and psychological violence that child sex crimes so often inflict.)

In the pages of the *Globe* Reeves also protested the formation of a police hotline that was created shortly after the Revere arrests. Believing that the problem of sexual molestation of children was not simply confined to the single locale of Revere, Suffolk County District Attorney Garrett H. Byrne set up a telephone number for people to call to report the suspected sexual molestation and rape of kids.

But to Reeves, the establishment of such a hotline amounted to – you guessed it – a "witch hunt" against the gay community.

Byrne's forces had arrested *over 200* gay men in the Boston area on sex crimes. And for this, the group denounced Byrne as "anti-gay" and loudly picketed a fundraiser for his re-election.[2]

Did the *Globe* ever once denounce Reeves for his shocking views on child molestation or ever challenge his claim that arresting men for sodomizing children was a "witch hunt against gay people"? No.

Rather, the *Globe* later published another supportive article of Reeves and his cause. Under the headline, "Gays optimistic about future of movement," Reeves reiterated that recent events and arrests in the Boston area over child sex crimes were an issue of "civil liberties."[3]

In a nutshell, the *Globe* became a *de facto* mouthpiece for Reeves and his crusade against the criminalization of sex between men and boys, even though it was found that many of the young victims came from broken homes or foster care.

And when D.A. Byrne was up for re-election in September of 1978, the *Globe* did not endorse Byrne as it had numerous times before. Instead, the editorial board aired qualms about Byrne's "civil-rights record" and asserted, "Byrne has to answer for the 'hot line' he tried to put into effect after the Revere sex scandal."[4] Amazingly, the language of the *Globe*'s editorial board was very similar with Reeves' "civil liberties" argument only months earlier in the paper.

Indeed, the *Boston Globe agreed* with the co-founder of NAMBLA that targeting child sex crimes was an issue of "civil liberties."

Days after the *Globe* editorial appeared, Byrne was defeated in his re-election bid. Thomas Reeves would later brag to a London writer about his resounding victory:

> "The old District Attorney (Byrne), who had brought the [Revere child sex] charges, was soundly defeated, partly due to the work of gay people. The new DA, after election, appeared on TV with me and said that no man need fear prison for sex involving a teenager unless coercion was involved … Many people – including gay people – had warned us that open gay work for so-called child molesters would backfire. It did not. It gave us strength."[5]

Truly, riding a wave of great publicity – provided in large part by the *Globe* – and revelling in the defeat of his chief political adversary, Reeves was empowered.

Only 12 weeks after the election, the North American Man/Boy Love Association was born.

"Fairness for all" = Sex with young boys?

Boise group's plea: Fairness for all

THOMAS REEVES

Six months before Thomas Reeves co-founded NAMBLA, the North American Man/Boy Love Association, the Boston Globe *gave Reeves a powerful forum to argue against the criminal prosecution of men having sex with underage boys. (The* Globe *headline is from April 17, 1978.)*

NOTES

[1] Thomas Reeves, "Boise group's plea: Fairness for all," *The Boston Globe*, April 17, 1978, p. 19.

[2] Fletcher Roberts, "Gay-rights group pickets outside Byrne fundraiser," *The Boston Globe*, April 28, 1978, p. 45. [Note: Burns lost re-election.]

[3] Teresa M. Hanafin, "Gays optimistic about future of movement," *The Boston Globe*, June 24, 1978, p. 27. [NOTE: Teresa Hanafin is now the editor of *Crux*, a web site launched by the *Boston Globe* in 2014 dedicated to "Covering all things Catholic." Go figure.]

[4] "Two races for district attorney" (editorial), *The Boston Globe*, September 12, 1978, p. 18.

[5] Tom O'Carroll, "Paedophilia: The Radical Case," *Contemporary Social Issues Series*, No. 12. London: Peter Owen, 1980. Chapter 13. (O'Carroll cites a "personal communication" with Reeves dated October, 8, 1979.)

12

Nude Children and Sadomasochism? No Problem at the *Globe*

In July of 1990, *The Perfect Moment*, an exhibition of photographs from New York City avant-garde photographer Robert Mapplethorpe, arrived for a showing at Boston's Institute of Contemporary Art (ICA) with great controversy.

Mapplethorpe was an openly gay man who had died of AIDS only a year earlier, and a number of the photographs in his collection contained shocking images of homosexual activity and sadomasochism. Many were outraged over photographs such as the one of a man urinating into the mouth of another. There was also the image of a man fully inserting his fist into another man's rectum.

Even before its contentious appearance in Boston, Mapplethorpe's exhibit unleashed a storm of debate over the public funding of art and the meaning of the word *obscene*. Previous exhibitions in other cities had already been cancelled, and in Cincinnati, the controversial exhibition resulted in a high-profile court case.[1]

Most notably, two of Mapplethorpe's photographs in his exhibition featured young children in a startling state of nudity. One photo featured a girl, probably about three-years-old, sitting in a dress on an outside bench with her legs wide open. Her dress was pulled up in such a way that her genitals were clearly exposed.

Another featured a totally nude young boy, probably about six-years-old, standing indoors upon the top of a sofa chair next to a refrigerator. (See edited photos on page 59.)

Some argued that the children's photos were hardly different from the kind of innocent, nude-in-the-bathtub, streaking-through-the-house fare that is found in many family photo albums. But such an argument ignored the larger sexual context of many of Mapplethorpe's photos, such as the graphic self-portrait of the photographer inserting a bullwhip into his anus.

What did the *Boston Globe* have to say about these photos of nude children being shown alongside graphic images of sadomasochism and homoeroticism?

In an article about the controversy, the *Globe*'s Mike Barnicle dismissed the photos as "marginal stuff" and "incredibly weird," and he made no mention at all of the troubling images of the nude children. He dubbed the debate over the Mapplethorpe exhibit "unbelievably embarrassing" and essentially argued that the country had more important issues to worry about.[2]

Meanwhile, after viewing the exhibit, *Globe* regular Bella English wrote, "For the most part, the exhibit is pretty benign." And then after asking, "What's the big deal?" English then suggested the uproar was over the fact that Mapplethorpe's images involved homosexuality and that the objection to his exhibit was really about attacking gay people.[3]

The same theme echoed a couple weeks later in an article in the *Globe* by Derrick Z. Jackson, who not-so-subtly tried to argue that the entire Mapplethorpe protest was about bigotry against the gay community. Jackson penned a story that uncritically relayed the claim of a gay man who said he was physically assaulted on his way to City Hall to protest the possible censorship of Mapplethorpe's exhibit.[4] Jackson's message was clear: Those who protested the Mapplethorpe exhibit were on the same platform as those who participated in public gay bashing.

Meanwhile, the *Globe* editorial board did not fare much better. While completely ignoring both the role of children in Mapplethorpe's photographs and the welfare of children altogether, a July 17, 1990, editorial simply argued that the federal government should continue to fund the arts "without restrictions" that "discourage artistic expression."[5]

A strong defense of children this was not. But by 1990, this was par for the course at the *Boston Globe.*

Another writer in Boston who did not have much of a problem with naked children in the Mapplethorpe exhibit was Margery Eagan over at the *Globe*'s crosstown rival, the *Boston Herald.*

According to Eagan, those who protested Mapplethorpe's photos were not well-meaning citizens defending decency and looking out for the welfare of children, but merely "artful dodgers" who were "very weird" and whose objections to the exhibit could be compared to the views of Adolf Hitler.[6]

Eagan also speculated that those who opposed Mapplethorpe's exhibit of naked children actually had sexual hang-ups of their own and should check themselves "into the nearest sexual deviance clinic."[7]

A month earlier, in June 1990, when gay activists hurled condoms at priests and their families at an ordination ceremony (see Chapter 7), Eagan used her column to profile a gay man who "understood the frustration" of those who committed the attacks. The acts were understandable, according to Eagan and her subject, because there was a "pathology within the Church."[8] This "pathology" was apparently due to the Church's recognition that sex between two or more guys is a sin.

Both the Catholic League and the Catholic Action League of Massachusetts would cite Eagan *numerous* times over the years for her fallacious and bleary-eyed attacks.[9]

In 2014, Eagan left her job at the *Herald* to become a "spirituality columnist" at Crux, a web site dedicated to "Covering all things Catholic."

Crux's hiring of Eagan was interesting, to say the least, in light of Eagan's noted record of dissent against the Church and the fact that she has often appeared to have a pretty weak grasp of what the Church actually teaches. For example, in an early column on Crux, Eagan wrongly informed her audience that the Catholic Church taught that a woman had "sinned" merely because her husband abandoned her.[10]

And the new title of "spirituality columnist" at a Catholic-themed site has never tempered Eagan's attacks on the Church. Continuing her ongoing tantrum against the teaching that homosexual acts are sinful and that two dudes making vows to each other is not a marriage, Eagan has been angrily espousing on Crux that the Church is "bigoted, backward, [and] blind" for not supporting "gay rights."[11]

Not only that, but Eagan has concluded that because of

the Church's doctrines on homosexual sex and the definition of marriage, "the Church may soon become the major defender of anti-gay bigotry in the world."[12]

Ultimately, however, seeing Margery Eagan as a "spirituality columnist" at Crux makes perfect sense in light of the company that owns and operates the site.

Crux is owned and operated by none other than … the *Boston Globe*.

How logical.

Nude kids and rectums O.K. at the *Boston Globe*

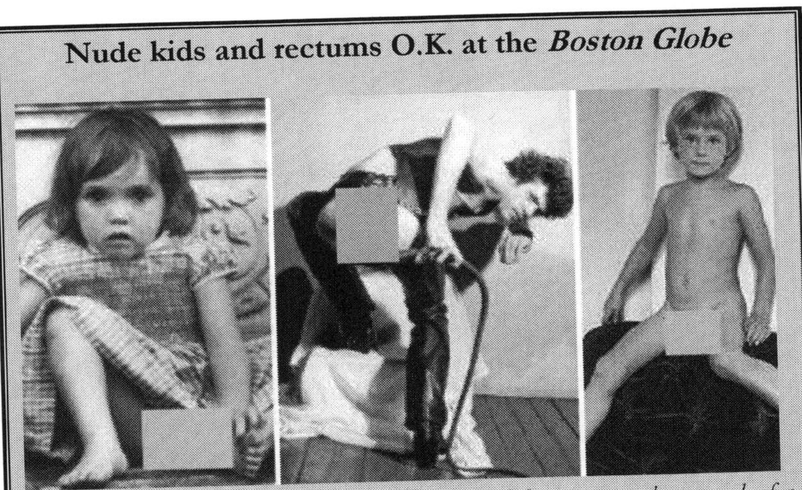

Looking out for the kids? The Boston Globe *did not seem to have much of a problem with images of naked children and gay sadomasochism shown together in a controversial 1990 Boston photo exhibit by artist Robert Mapplethorpe.*

NOTES

[1] Isabel Wilkerson, "Cincinnati jury acquits museum in Mapplethorpe obscenity case," *The Boston Globe*, October 6, 1990.
[2] Mike Barnicle, "Things obscene and not heard," *The Boston Globe*, August 2, 1990, p. 17.
[3] Bella English, "Censor futility at the museum," *The Boston Globe*, August 1, 1990, p. 17.
[4] Derrick Z. Jackson, "Walking in their shoes," *The Boston Globe*, August 17, 1990, p. 25.
[5] "Funding, not policing, the arts" (editorial), *The Boston Globe*, July 17, 1990, p. 12.
[6] Margery Eagan, "Artful dodgers give their meaning of 'Common Sense'," *The Boston Herald*, August 2, 1990, p. 8.
[7] Margery Eagan, "Dwelling on Mapplethorpe hides the bigger picture," *The Boston Herald*, July 31, 1990, p. 10.
[8] Margery Eagan, "The anger, compassion of a gay Catholic man," *The Boston Herald*, June 19, 1990, p. 10.
[9] The Catholic League for Religious and Civil Rights is led by Dr. Bill Donohue in New York City. The Catholic Action League of Massachusetts is spearheaded by C.J. Doyle in Boston.
[10] Margery Eagan, "My 'aunt' was abandoned by her husband. What was her sin, exactly?" Crux.com, October 8, 2014. Here is what the Catechism of the Catholic Church (CCC) states in its section on divorce: "It can happen that one of the spouses is the innocent victim of a divorce decreed by civil law; this spouse therefore **has not contravened the moral law**. There is a considerable difference between a spouse who has sincerely tried to be faithful to the sacrament of marriage and is **unjustly abandoned**, and one who through his own grave fault destroys a canonically valid marriage" (CCC 2386).
[11] Margery Eagan, "How can those who support gay rights remain in the Church?" Crux.com, July 1, 2015. [See also: Margery Eagan, "My prayer: That Francis prevails over the bigots within the Church," Crux.com, October 21, 2014.]
[12] Margery Eagan, "Anti-gay bias: Is this really where the Church wants to be?" Crux.com, May 6, 2015.

13

Church in the Crosshairs

Slapping the tag "anti-Catholic" onto a newspaper column or a media outlet merely because it criticizes the Catholic Church is neither fair nor appropriate. True anti-Catholicism manifests itself as an open contempt for the teachings and practices of the faith. True anti-Catholicism disparages and insults those who adhere to Church teachings as being less enlightened, less intelligent, and less attractive.

And when a clear and honest assessment is applied, there is no question that the *Boston Globe* has distinguished itself as a virulently anti-Catholic newspaper.

Although it would be tough to pinpoint an exact moment when the *Globe*'s antagonism began, Boston Catholics began to take notice of the paper's growing hostility toward the Church in the mid-1970s.

For example, in October of 1976, the *Globe*'s ombudsman, Charles L. Whipple, felt compelled to respond to a deluge of angry phone calls and letters from local Catholics concerning a recent political cartoon by Paul Szep and a column by Mike Barnicle.

Szep had published a cartoon featuring a depiction of Pope Paul VI that imagined the pontiff's reaction to a recent victory in an Italian election of Christian Democrats over Communists. Whipple knew that most people did not object to the political point being made, but he acknowledged that he "knew instinctively there would be complaints" as soon as he saw the "dwarfish depiction" of the Pope looking like "Dopey the Dwarf" which "grossly exceed the bounds of fairness" and contained a "component of cruelty."[1]

Whipple also understood complaints with the column by Barnicle, which mused over the alleged lack of political sex scandals in Massachusetts. "For one thing," Barnicle had written, "most of the women working on Beacon Hill and City Hall probably went to parochial school and, thus, have a very deep fear of sex ... This same fear also has a grip on many of the men."

"For obvious reasons of fairness," concluded Whipple, "we think the desk editor should have penciled out that paragraph." And as for Szep's cartoon of Pope Paul VI, it "should have been dispensed with wholly," he added.[2]

In a short time, however, these offending pieces in 1976 would seem tame in comparison to what the *Globe* would later unleash. For the next three decades, the *Globe* would repeatedly and relentlessly bludgeon and belittle faithful Catholics while celebrating those who publically rejected the Church and its teachings.

On May 28, 1978, the *Globe* published an especially ugly article, "Legacy of the ex-Catholic," which gleefully profiled those who had no longer practiced Catholicism. In doing so, the *Globe* essentially treated Catholicism as if it were a mental disorder from which there was little hope of recovery. So traumatized were some former Catholics, claimed the *Globe*, that they were mired "in therapy for years." After harping over "the tendency of among ex-Catholics to trade horror stories, to see who can come up with the worst atrocity committed at the hands of some sadistic monsignor or mother superior," the *Globe* asked, "Have lives been ruined, sex made miserable, guilts been exaggerated?"[3]

The article also profiled a nameless ex-Catholic who was "sometimes disdainful" of the faith but still sent his kids to CCD classes every week. Why? "[T]o give them something of their own to rebel against," the doctor replied "with a rueful grin."

And what was the cause of this terrible mental affliction, according to the article? Well, the *Globe* quoted a "downtown priest" who "conceded that the church could have come up sooner with more enlightened attitudes on questions like birth control, the question which many ex-Catholics feel triggered their alienation from Catholicism."[4]

A-ha. So, according to the *Globe*, Catholics who disagreed with the paper's editorial board on birth control were somehow less "enlightened" than everyone else.

Only a couple months later the *Globe* followed up with a feature article, "Ex-Nun Who Married an FBI Chief," which told the story of Shirley Kelley, the wife of then-FBI Director Clarence M. Kelley. The *Globe* beamed that Shirley had been "unfulfilled" and "totally, boringly saturated" in her life as a nun wearing her traditional habit and living in a convent. After leaving the cloistered life, Kelley then "dated some of Washington's most famous politicians" before marrying the head of the FBI.

In the end, concluded the Globe, *Kelley* "sounds less and less like an ex-nun and more and more like an emancipated woman glorying in her liberation."[5]

A year later, the *Globe* took everything a step further. Not only was Catholicism a hindrance to "liberation," it was *dangerous*! At least that was the message from a September 26, 1979, article with the title, "Do women fit in the Catholic Church? Not with God as Almighty *Father*" by Karen Lindsey.

According to Lindsey, women had no chance for happy lives inside the Catholic Church, especially if they had attended Catholic schools as children. Lindsey's characterization of Catholic schools was similar to a depiction of Alcatraz Island.

"Guilt and terror – the staples of a good Catholic education," Lindsey chimed. "And it was subsidized by an invasion of privacy that the sternest police state would envy." And while denigrating the Virgin Mary as "an ideal of psychotic passivity," Lindsey then asserted her Catholic school upbringing had "created a system of unreality that poorly prepared us for adulthood."[6]

In the eyes of Lindsey, nothing could free a woman from the clutches of the Church, except lots of sex, contraception, and unfettered access to abortion. And a choice in opposition to this lifestyle – the life of a nun, for example – was simply an abomination. Lindsey quoted "Vicky, a former nun," who described her formation in the convent as a "thoroughgoing destruction of human beings."

In ensuing years, the *Globe* would *repeatedly* portray ex-Catholics and dissenting Catholics as somehow being more "enlightened" and "liberated" than pious Catholics.

A 1981 profile of artist Corita Kent, for example, continued this ongoing motif. Kent left her life as a nun, reported the *Globe*, because she had "moved beyond the boundaries of the Catholic faith."

"For me, there just came a time that it seemed I could operate better without all that," the *Globe* gladly quoted Kent.

"It was just a natural growth … I see it as the sort of growing up that we are all asked to do."[7] Again, the clear message from the *Globe* was that those who were actually faithful to the Catholic Church had not yet "grown up."

By the early 1980s, Boston Catholics began to take notice of the paper's open and relentless hostility. So pervasive and glaring was the *Globe*'s animus against the Catholic Church that Robert P. Largess, writing for The Catholic League for Religious and Civil Rights, authored a book in 1983 entitled, *Keeping Catholics in Their Place: The Boston Globe's Cultural Imperialism*.[8]

In page after page, Largess cites numerous cases to support the charge that the *Globe* had become an unapologetically anti-Catholic newspaper.[9] And the remarkable aspect of the book is that Largess' study covered only a relatively short period of time, from 1978 to 1981. After several compelling chapters with many examples supporting his premise, Largess summed up his study in his last chapter:

> "[T]he *Globe* has published dozens of articles per year attacking the Pope, the bishops, Cardinal [Humberto] Medeiros, priests, lay people, Catholic ethnic groups, Catholic morals, and Catholic opposition to birth control, to abortion, to divorce, to premarital sex, and to homosexuality … Catholics have been accused of undermining our society, breaking down the wall of separation of church and state, authoritarianism, repression, fascism, warped minds, collective psychosis, and lying."[10]

Indeed, Largess openly acknowledged that the *Globe* could not be tagged as being anti-Catholic merely for disagreeing with the Church for its teachings. But the relentlessness and mean-spirited double standard with which it unleashed its assault could not be ignored.

For example, in the months leading up to the 1980 elections, Largess counted no less than 36 articles from the *Globe* attacking Boston's Cardinal Medeiros. In September of 1980, Medeiros issued a letter to Boston-area Catholics reminding them of their moral responsibility of their votes at election time and that the issue of abortion should play an essential role at the ballot box.[11] (At the time, there were over 1.5 million surgical abortions per year in the United States, significantly more than there are now.)

Day after day the *Globe*'s message to its readers was that Medeiros' call to Catholics was somehow "disturbing" and a danger to democracy. Typical of the *Globe*'s attack on the Church was the September 18, 1980, article, "Too much church? – that's the question." You can guess what the answer was.

Meanwhile, the *Globe*'s Mike Barnicle went after Cardinal Medeiros and fretted that somehow, "A bumper sticker with an actual candidate's name on it could thus be an actual sin."[12]

Then there was the September 20, 1980, article, which began, "As a pastor seeking to lay a guilt trip on his flock, Humberto Cardinal Medeiros is a flop."[13] Not surprisingly, the assessment of the cardinal did not get much better after that.

A few days later, *Globe* columnist Ellen Goodman weighed in with the column, "Moral peril at the polls." Her conclusion? "Churches are becoming the new Tammany Hall of the 1980s."[14] Eek.

Legacy of the ex-Catholic

May 28, 1978

The ex-nun who married an FBI chief

July 14, 1978

'Once a Catholic' is irreverent, irresistible

August 22, 1979

'Too much church?' — that's the question

September 18, 1980

Do women fit in the Catholic Church?

Not with God as Almighty *Father*

September 26, 1979

Cartoonist Paul Szep

Paul Szep was the chief editorial cartoonist at the Boston Globe *for several decades until 2001. The teachings of the Catholic Church were often in Szep's crosshairs over the years. In 1983, Szep won the renowned Thomas Nast Prize, named after the famed 19th century cartoonist Thomas Nast, a well-known anti-Catholic. (Top from 5/17/1991; bottom from 11/20/1992.)*

Paul Szep (con'd)

Boston-area Catholics would have a hard time ignoring Szep's ugly caricatures of Catholic leaders over the years. (Pope John Paul II from 3/6/1992; Pope Paul VI from 6/23/1976; Cardinal Law from 1/11/1995.)

Cartoonist Dan Wasserman

Dan Wasserman has been an editorial cartoonist at the Globe *since 1985. As with Paul Szep, the Catholic Church has been a popular target. (Top from 3/12/1987; bottom from 8/15/1994.)*

NOTES

1 Charles L. Whipple, "Szep's cartoon and Barnicle's column," *The Boston Globe*, July 1, 1976, p. 21.

2 Ibid.

3 Otile McManus, "Legacy of the ex-Catholic," *The Boston Globe*, May 28, 1978, p. 43.

4 Ibid.

5 Marian Christy, "The ex-nun who married an FBI chief, *The Boston Globe*, July 14, 1978.

6 Karen Lindsey, "Do women fit in the Catholic Church? Not with God as almighty *Father*," *The Boston Globe*, September 26, 1979, p. 69.

7 Nina McCain. "The world is her paint brush – and her colors are bright," *The Boston Globe*, August 15, 1981, p. 2.

8 Robert P. Largess (1983). *Keeping Catholics in Their Place: The Boston Globe's Cultural Imperialism*. Milwaukee: The Catholic League for Religious and Civil Rights.

9 I cited a few of Largess' examples above (Legacy of the ex-Catholic article; ex-nun who became wife of FBI guy; Corita Kent).

10 Largess.

11 "Text of the Medeiros Letter," *The Boston Globe*, September 12, 1980, p. 22.

12 Mike Barnicle, "A letter, an issue, a memory," *The Boston Globe*, September 15, 1980, p. 21.

13 Colman McCarthy, "Guilt trip a flop," *The Boston Globe*, September 20, 1980, p. 15.

14 Ellen Goodman, "Moral peril at the polls," *The Boston Globe*, September 23, 1980, p. 11.

14

Rave Reviews

By the 1970s, Hollywood's portrayal decades earlier of the archetypal Catholic priest as Bing Crosby in *The Bells of St. Mary's* had long disappeared. Whereas attacks on Catholic priests and Catholic teaching were once rare, the 1970s witnessed Hollywood forces and countercultural artists becoming bold in attacking the Catholic Church.

And at this time, the *Boston Globe* was more-than-willing to promote just about any and all attacks on the Church that it became aware of.

In August of 1978, a local theater company staged *Once a Catholic*, a play that was fearless in ridiculing Catholic teaching and Catholic religious. And even though the nearest offering of the play was at a theater on Cape Cod, hours away from the *Globe*'s offices in Boston, the distance did not stop the *Globe* theater critic Kevin Kelly from running to check it out and bestow a glowing review.

Once a Catholic centered around Mary Mooney, a 15-year-old attending a parochial school and apparently feeling the need to ask blunt questions in class about the female reproductive system to her teacher, Mother Basil, a stammering nun. Kelly beamed that this "attack on Catholic teaching at the dropsical hands of nuns" was "exhilarating in its sacrilege" and "wondrously anti-clerical."[1]

"Without question, you should see it," pleaded Kelly. Whether the play would offend faithful Catholics was not a concern at all to Kelly. In fact, the play's "exhilarating" attack on the Church was something to be celebrated.

A few years later, in 1981, the notorious anti-Catholic play, *Sister Mary Ignatius Explains It All For You*, made its first appearance. Penned by the openly gay ex-Catholic Christopher Durang, whose "faith started to fade when he was attending Harvard Divinity School,"[2] the play is of a callous and angry nun lecturing her audience on Catholic teaching. However, the faith is reduced to nothing less than simple idiocy and outright barbarity. The climax of the play arrives when Mary pulls a gun from her habit and then murders her pupils.

The Catholic League For Religious and Civil Rights would later describe it as "one of the most anti-Catholic plays ever written," and even Jewish and interreligious organizations joined in condemning the play.[3]

Some critics across the country, such as Lloyd Rose at the *Washington Post*, could see through the bile and tagged the play as Durang's "hate letter to the Catholic Church" and a "splenetic response to his years as a gay teenager in Catholic schools."[4]

But needless to say, the *Boston Globe*'s Kelly saw it a bit differently. Though he quibbled with the direction of the plot, Kelly raved that "Durang's play is bull's-eye perfect, coruscating satire scored from the reality of the Catholic Church." He also hailed the actress in the lead role for her "perfect, mouth-worming, paranoiac characterization."[5]

A couple years later, in 1983, in a fawning interview with

Durang, Kelly reminded *Globe* readers that *Sister Mary Ignatius* was a "savage, satirical attack on Catholic education" that was "blistering and funny."[6] And then two years later, in 1985, while still defending the play against charges that it was an attack on the Catholic Church, Kelly again asserted, "Durang's rage is not anti-Catholic; it's not that limited."[7]

And even a decade after his first review, in 1991, Kelly was still praising *Sister Mary Ignatius* when it returned to Boston for yet another run. In a review entitled, "Devilish Good Fun With Sister Mary," Kelly raved that the "Catholic-snapping satire" was "a tour de force that sparkles like votive lights in a dark church echoing with laughter – ours."[8]

In the end, from the late 1970s into the 21st century, Catholics became accustomed to witnessing *Globe* reviewers regularly shower praises upon works that castigated the Catholic Church. In 1999, a letter to the *Globe* from one reader pretty much summed up the feelings of many Catholics in the Boston area:

> "[E]vidence of anti-Catholic bias over the years at the *Globe* would be evident to anyone who takes the trouble to search back issues. This bias has appeared over the years in vicious anti-Catholic cartoons, and film, theater, television, book reviews and elsewhere in the form of snide remarks. A play, movie, TV program or book that attacks the Catholic Church, or ridicules its teachings, is guaranteed a favorable review by *Globe* writers. Letters in rebuttal are rarely published."[9]

Although a work attacking the Church was certainly not "guaranteed" a positive review, the reader was entirely correct that Catholics could not help but notice that *Globe* reviewers often celebrated such pieces. What follows is just a small sample of how the *Globe* assessed some notoriously anti-Catholic works:

- *Mass Appeal* (1980 play): This stage production about a narrow-minded, alcoholic priest and a bisexual seminarian clearly had Church teachings about sexuality and the all-male priesthood in its crosshairs. At one point, the priest advises the seminarian, "If you want to become a priest, lie."[10] Yet the *Globe*'s Kevin Kelly raved that it was "a fast funny, fierce, philosophical slugfest" and "an exhilarating play, one of the best of this or any other year." There was not a syllable in Kelly's review that Catholics might be offended.[11]

- *The Last Temptation of Christ* (1988): Martin Scorsese's vision of a wild-eyed and befuddled Jesus Christ was not only met by angry nationwide protests, it was dubbed as "one of the most blasphemous films ever produced."[12] Yet the *Globe*'s Jay Carr not only disparaged those who criticized the movie but beamed that it was a "powerful and serious film by a serious film maker" and a "gritty, deeply felt effort."[13]

- *The Boys of St. Vincent* (1993): The 1995 Boston Gay & Lesbian Film/Video Festival trumpeted this film about Catholic priests sexually abusing children.[14] So offensive was the film that even one of the most liberal papers in the country, New York's *The Village Voice*, saw that it was "programmed to offend."[15] Yet the *Globe*'s Michael Blowen lauded it as "riveting" and fretted that this "sensation" had not found a larger audience.[16]

- *Priest* (1995): This notoriously warped film about a pair of sexually active priests (one of whom is gay, of course) is "arguably the most anti-Catholic movie ever made," said Jewish film critic Michael Medved.[17] The film's director openly admitted that *Priest* was "against a hierarchy adhering to old-fashioned rules without looking at the way the world's changed."[18] Even the liberal *Los Angeles Times* saw that the film was "an angry piece of invective directed at the Catholic Church's hierarchy." Yet *Globe* film critic Jay Carr unbelievably tried to twist the aim of the film by actually claiming that the film "pays Catholicism the compliment of taking it seriously." He then added that *Priest* had "heart, power, immediacy and a spiritual imperative."[19] One wonders if Carr would have had the same feelings toward a similar movie with the title, *Rabbi.*

- *Dogma* (1999): This warped "comedy," which imagined God as a woman and a descendant of Jesus as an abortion clinic worker, was so obviously offensive that one media outlet opined, "If members of the Catholic League don't picket this one, they're comatose."[20] Yet the *Globe*'s Carr stepped up once again to rave that *Dogma* was a "sweet" film that "only a sincere believer could make."[21] Uh-huh.

- *The Magdalene Sisters* (2003): This vulgar film's central premise, that the Catholic Church in Ireland operated homes for troubled youth that were rife with unspeakable barbarity and unrivaled cruelty from the nuns who operated them, has now been proven to be *completely false.*[22] Yet *Globe* critic Ty Burr beamed that this gross attack on the Church was a "blistering and brilliant work of true-life moral agitprop" and "the best movie I've seen so far this year."[23]

NOTES

[1] Kevin Kelly, "'Once a Catholic' is irreverent, irresistible," *The Boston Globe*, August 22, 1979, p. 54.
[2] "Losing His Religion" ("Names & Faces" feature), *The Boston Globe*, May 25, 2001, p. D4.
[3] Bill Donohue, "Variety Ad Makes Appeal to Viacom's Sumner Redstone," The Catholic League for Religious and Civil Rights, news release, May 14, 2001.
[4] Lloyd Rose, "Scena's Vexatious 'Ignatius'," *The Washington Post*, August 9, 1996, p. B3.
[5] Kevin Kelly, "Fine satire, but poor melodrama: *Sister Mary Ignatius Explains It All For You* and *The Actor's Nightmare*; by Christopher Durang," *The Boston Globe*, November 14, 1981, p. 14.
[6] Kevin Kelly, "Mischief lurks under dramatist's angelic mien," *The Boston Globe*, March 27, 1983.
[7] Kevin Kelly, "The halos under challenge: Catholics and the playwright," *The Boston Globe*, March 10, 1985, p. A1.
[8] Kevin Kelly, "Devilish Good Fun with Sister Mary," *The Boston Globe*, July 18, 1991, p. 71.
[9] Richard F. Russo (Arlington, Mass.) "Publishing Catholic viewpoint was overdue" (Letter to the Editor), *The Boston Globe*, December 13, 1999, p. A17. (Russo was responding to an earlier letter by C.J. Doyle of the Catholic Action League of Massachusetts, published on December 1, 1999, which criticized the *Globe*'s treatment of the Church.)
[10] Catholic League for Religious and Civil Rights, *2006 Report on Anti-Catholicism*, The Arts.
[11] Kevin Kelly, "Mass Appeal a work of high art," *The Boston Globe*, August 28, 1980; also by Kelly, "Mass Appeal has real mass appeal," October 7, 1981.
[12] "Bravo Hosts 'Last Temptation'," The Catholic League for Religious and Civil Rights (*Catalyst*), September 1998.
[13] Jay Carr, "A powerful, sincere look at Christ, *The Boston Globe*, September 2, 1988, p. 25.
[14] Matthew Gilbert, "Gay, lesbian fest sets lineup," *The Boston Globe*, May 7, 1995, p. 41.
[15] Bill Donohue, "A&E to air another critical show on Catholic

Church," The Catholic League for Religious and Civil Rights, news release, February 9, 1995.

16 Michael Blowen, "Thoughtful, tough 'Boys'," *The Boston Globe*, February 17, 1995, p. 33.

17 Bill Donohue (2005) *Secular Sabotage: How Liberals Are Destroying Religion and Culture in America* (New York: FaithWords).

18 Ibid.

19 Jay Carr, "Soul-searching 'Priest' reveals impassioned humanity," *The Boston Globe*, April 7, 1995, p. 89.

20 "Disney dumps 'Dogma'; Movie, protest proceed," The Catholic League for Religious and Civil Rights (*Catalyst*), May 1999.

21 Jay Carr, "Earnest 'Dogma' a film to believe in," *The Boston Globe*, November 12, 1999, p. D1.

22 In February of 2013, the Irish government released the independent McAleese Report, which sought to examine the country's role in the Magdalene laundries, which operated for over two centuries until 1996. The findings were indeed eye-opening. Of the many scores of women who were interviewed for the report, exactly ***zero*** reported being sexually abused by a nun. None. Nada. Zilch. A woman quoted in the report exclaimed, "It has shocked me to read in papers that we were beat and our heads shaved and that we were badly treated by the nuns … I was not touched by any nun and I never saw anyone touched." For more, see Brendan O'Neill, "Catholic-bashers have embellished the truth about abuse in Catholic institutions. It's time to put the record straight," *The Telegraph* (UK), http://blogs.telegraph.co.uk, February 14, 2013 and "The Truth About Ireland's Magdalene Laundries," TheMediaReport.com, February 19, 2013.

23 Ty Burr, "Prisoners of faith: 'Sisters' is a gripping look at horror of Ireland's asylums," *The Boston Globe*, August 15, 2003, p. C1.

15

The *Globe*'s Kind of (Ex-)Priest

"While we have to be very cautious in applying the anti-Catholic label to self-described Catholics, on occasion the term is applicable." – Sociologist Philip Jenkins[1]

After the publication of Robert Largess' 1983 analysis of the *Boston Globe*, entitled *Keeping Catholics in Their Place* (from Chapter 13), many Boston-area Catholics must have thought that the paper would reassess its coverage of the Catholic Church and its treatment of faithful Catholics.

Such observers would soon be disappointed. Eileen McNamara, Joan Vennochi, Derrick Z. Jackson, Kevin Cullen, Bella English, David Nyhan, Charles Pierce, Maureen Dezell, Ellen Goodman, and Mike Barnicle are all writers for the *Globe* who would be cited over the years by either the watchdog groups the Catholic League and/or the Catholic Action League of Massachusetts for their warped attacks on the Catholic Church. Needless to say, the editorial board of the *Globe* would be repeatedly noted as well.

However, it would be an angry ex-priest by the name of

James Carroll who would ultimately set the gold standard for anti-Catholic attacks in the *Globe* and eventually have many asking if Carroll was indeed "the biggest anti-Catholic bigot on the block."[2]

The Church ordained Carroll as a Paulist priest in 1969, and he served as "Catholic Chaplain" at Boston University until 1974, when "he left the priesthood to become a writer."[3] After writing some listless novels, Carroll began contributing some articles to the *Globe* in the 1980s. In 1992 – when the *Globe* unleashed its first blitzkrieg of reporting on sex abuse in the Catholic Church – Carroll became a regular columnist for the *Globe*.

No charge or urban legend has ever been too wild for Carroll to propagate, whether it be blaming Pope Pius XII for the proliferation of the Holocaust,[4] accusing the Church of "anti-Muslim bigotry,"[5] or implicating the Church for modern-day anti-Semitism in the United States. Carroll's venomous and over-the-top attacks against the Church cannot be overstated.

In fact, even as recently as 2014, Carroll unleashed a truly bizarre charge claiming that even *today* he still hears "anti-Jewish stereotypes" in the pews. "I still hear such (anti-Jewish) preaching at least once a month," claimed Carroll.[6] Such a charge would be shocking if it were true. But Carroll did not care to tell his audience *where* he allegedly heard such venomous language. Let's just say most Boston-area Catholics would be highly skeptical of Carroll's ferocious claim.

And regarding Carroll's warped history regarding the Church and the Holocaust, Jewish historian Rabbi David G. Dalin has written:

"[E]x-priests like James Carroll [and] other lapsed or

> angry liberal Catholics exploit the tragedy of the Jewish people during the Holocaust to foster their own political agenda of forcing changes on the Catholic Church today. This hijacking of the Holocaust must be repudiated."[7]

And after studying Carroll's works and one of his books, esteemed sociologist Philip Jenkins at Baylor University has concluded that Carroll essentially "rejects virtually the whole of Christian theology" and "advocates a total change in the nature" of the Church.

"For Carroll," Jenkins determined, "the Church is founded upon hatred and is in every sense a hateful institution."[8]

Even the precious days of Holy Week and Easter Sunday have been the target of Carroll's bile. According to the *Globe*'s Carroll, the Gospel accounts of Jesus' death and Resurrection are not the heart and center of Christian life but "an immorality tale of hate."[9]

And if one ever thought that the Virgin Mary would be safe from Carroll's contempt, one would see that he actually once referred to the Holy Mother as "the mascot of her gender's subjugation."[10]

C.J. Doyle of the Catholic Action League of Massachusetts has tirelessly cited Carroll *numerous* times over the years for his erroneous and noxious attacks, and he has noted Carroll's "obsessive, decades-long campaign to defame and discredit the Catholic Faith."[11]

But then again, this is the *Boston Globe*. As Doyle has observed:

> "No other religion is made the object of such continuous venom in the pages of the *Globe*. No other denomination must suffer one of its ex-ministers repeatedly declaiming

its alleged derelictions in a major American newspaper."[12]

NOTES

[1] Jenkins, Philip, *The new anti-Catholicism: The last acceptable prejudice* (2003). New York: Oxford University Press. p. 15.
[2] William A. Donohue, Ph.D. "The biggest anti-Catholic bigot on the block?" *Catalyst* (the publication of The Catholic League for Religious and Civil Rights), December 2000.
[3] From www.jamescarroll.net.
[4] TheMediaReport.com, "James Carroll Exploits Holocaust, Lies Again About Catholic Church," December, 26, 2009.
[5] TheMediaReport.com, "Boston Globe's Carroll Busted For Airing Bogus History," April 11, 2011.
[6] Carroll, James. (2014) Excerpt from *Christ actually: The Son of God for the Secular Age*, Penguin Group (USA) LLC. at www.cruxnow.com/faith/2014/10/27/god-is-love-but-love-is-tied-to-suffering/
[7] Dalin, David G. (2002). *The myth of Hitler's pope*. Washington, D.C., Regnery History, pp. 2-3.
[8] Jenkins, p. 15.
[9] James Carroll, "The wicked irony of Holy Week," *The Boston Globe*, March 30, 2015, p. A9.
[10] As cited by C.J. Doyle, "Vichy Catholic," at http://www.catholicculture.org/culture/library/view.cfm?recnum=2873 (*Very* highly recommended).
[11] Catholic Action League of Massachusetts letter to the editor of *The Boston Globe*, by C.J. Doyle, March 31, 2015.
[12] Ibid.

16

"Puff, the Magic Felony"

In 1969, Peter Yarrow was riding high as one third of the popular folk group Peter, Paul and Mary. Songs including "Puff, the Magic Dragon," "If I Had a Hammer," and "Leaving on a Jet Plane" had become radio staples.

Yet in the midst of Yarrow's immense success, police in Washington, D.C. arrested him on shocking underage sex charges. On August 31, 1969, Yarrow was in D.C. for a series of his group's concerts, and a 17-year-old girl, allegedly the president of the group's fan club, and her 14-year-old sister went to visit Yarrow at the Shoreham Hotel.[1]

When he greeted the pair at the door, Yarrow was completely naked.[2] The young girls came for an autograph, but Yarrow had other ideas. "Put your books on the shelf," he told the pair.[3]

Yarrow then coerced the 14-year-old to perform oral sex on him, which she eventually did.

Yarrow pleaded guilty to the crime, which could have landed him ten years in jail. But with some powerful political connections (Yarrow's wife was the niece of the famed Eugene McCarthy), Yarrow only had to serve a mere three *months* behind bars.[4]

The family of the girls also sued Yarrow, accusing the singer of "seduction, assault and battery, and enticing and harboring" the girls over a three-year period, from 1966 to 1969.[5]

Yet Yarrow's career continued unabated by his pesky conviction on child molestation charges. (Yarrow even performed publicly between his arrest and his sentencing.[6]) Peter, Paul, and Mary continued to enjoy several years of touring to adoring fans, and Yarrow even pursued solo projects including one, ironically, of a children's book.[7]

However, the most eye-opening event of this entire episode may have occurred in the early days of 1981, when President Jimmy Carter, in the waning days of his administration, actually *pardoned* Yarrow for his underage sex crimes.[8]

Yet Yarrow's crimes have never been much of a concern to the *Boston Globe*. His arrest and sentencing merited only passing mentions in the news "brief" sections. And when Jimmy Carter pardoned Yarrow, the *Globe* did not even publish a syllable of concern about a President excusing a convicted child molester.

In ensuing years, Peter, Paul and Mary would make a number of concert appearances in the Boston area, and the *Globe* was almost always there to review them, with Yarrow's child sex crimes long forgotten.

In 1982, the *Globe* never questioned a U.S. Senate candidate in Massachusetts by the name of John Kerry about why he employed Yarrow to perform at his fundraisers.[9]

And over the years the *Boston Globe* has never asked why WGBH-TV, the local Boston affiliate of PBS, the national public television network, has repeatedly aired *Peter, Paul &*

Mary: Carry It On: A Musical Legacy, a fawning 80-minute retrospective of the group, which conveniently leaves out Yarrow's unflattering criminal episode.

If Peter Yarrow were ever *Father* Peter Yarrow, a Catholic priest, would the *Globe* ever have excused and forgotten Yarrow's crimes?

Not a chance.

NOTES

1 Evan Thomas, *The Man to See* (New York: Simon and Schuster, 1991), p. 255.
2 "Folk Singer Pleads Guilty in Sex Case" (UPI), *The Chicago Tribune*, March 27, 1970.
3 Scott McCabe, "Famous D.C. child sex offender profiting on book for new generation of kids," dccrimestories.com, August 1, 2013.
4 Thomas, p. 256.
5 McCabe. McCabe reports that he does not know the outcome of the civil suit.
6 John Darnton, "20,000 Youths Attend Rock 'Festival for Peace' Here," *The New York Times*, August 7, 1970.
7 Peter Yarrow, Lenny Lipton, *Puff, the Magic Dragon* (New York: Sterling Publishing, 2007).
8 Thomas; McCabe.
9 "Short Circuits," *The Boston Globe*, August 22, 1982.

17

Not Very Funny

On June 27, 2001, California police arrested and charged popular stand-up comic Paula Poundstone, who grew up in the Boston suburb of Sudbury, on three shocking counts of committing a lewd and lascivious act on a girl under the age of 14 and one count of child endangerment.

The felony complaint declared that Poundstone committed her crimes "willfully, unlawfully, and lewdly … with the intent of arousing, appealing to, and gratifying [her] lust, passions, and sexual desires."[1]

To avoid jail time, Poundstone later pleaded no contest to one count of felony child abuse and a misdemeanor count of "inflicting injury upon a child."

The court records were sealed, but unlike with cases involving Catholic priests, there was no outcry by anyone at the *Boston Globe* over the secret proceedings or a demand that the records be made public. No one from the *Globe*'s "Spotlight Team" went running to a judge to demand that they see the records.

Rather, within months of Poundstone's shocking charges, the *Globe* was showering the felon-comic with affection. In March 2002, while the paper was in the midst of its most brutal reporting lambasting the Catholic Church, the *Globe* trumpeted two fawning articles of Poundstone.

A *Globe* review of a local performance beamed, "Poundstone has never been funnier,"[2] while the paper entitled a second profile of the comic, "Poundstone finds that she can laugh after tragedy, tears."[3]

Felony abuse charges? Hilarious?

(Today, Paula Poundstone entertains audiences on *Wait Wait ... Don't Tell Me*, the popular weekly quiz show airing on a Boston radio affiliate of National Public Radio (NPR). And as a popular figure on the stand-up comedy circuit for over three decades, Poundstone performs in the neighborhood of 200 stand-up comedy shows per year around the nation.)

NOTES

[1] Felony complaint for arrest warrant, Case #SA042407, Superior Court of the State of California for the County of Los Angeles, June 27, 2001.

[2] Nick A. Zaino, III, "Poundstone returns with humor intact," *The Boston Globe*, March 23, 2002, p. D8.

[3] Jim Sullivan, "Poundstone finds that she can laugh after tragedy, tears," *The Boston Globe*, March 20, 2002, p. F1.

18

The *Phoenix*, not the *Globe*

When the story of Catholic sex abuse is told, many will often say that the story began on Sunday, January 6, 2002, the day of the first of hundreds of stories that year by the *Boston Globe*.

What many people do not know, however, is that much of the *Globe*'s early coverage that year – including the paper's first 2002 article, "Church allowed abuse by priest for years" – was remarkably similar to work that appeared nearly a year earlier in another paper in Boston: the *Boston Phoenix*.

The *Boston Phoenix* began in the mid-1960s as a cutting-edge weekly newspaper catering to the arts and entertainment community. (Imagine Boston's version of *The Village Voice*.) Blossoming under the leadership of Stephen Mindich in the 1970s, the paper was also known for its large area devoted to "adult-oriented" advertisements (escort services, etc.).

On March 23, 2001 – nearly *ten months* before the *Globe*'s first articles in 2002 – the *Phoenix* featured the first of a series of blistering front-page stories written by investigative writer Kristen Lombardi about the Archdiocese of Boston and its approach to clergy abuse cases. Lombardi's first article, "Cardinal Sin: Cardinal Law, the Church, and Pedophilia" ran an astonishing 6,700 words and gave a lengthy – albeit slanted and not completely accurate[1] – account of the Church's handling of the abusive John Geoghan and the devastating effect that Geoghan's abuse had on his victims. In subsequent months, Lombardi would author other articles of similar length and breadth about the scandals.

In imagining how the *Globe* "Spotlight Team" decided to launch its series of articles about Catholic sex abuse, one cannot help but picture *Globe* staffers like Walter Robinson, Michael Rezendes, Sacha Pfeiffer, and Matt Carroll at the paper's offices in the summer of 2001 with the *Phoenix* spread out on a table and crafting a plan to advance Lombardi's story.

Indeed, the *Globe*'s early 2002 articles featured a number of the exact same sources that Lombardi had already used a year earlier. Writer Jason Berry, Fr. Tom Doyle, and ex-priest Richard Sipe were all a major part of Lombardi's landmark first article and also played a prominent role in the *Globe*'s other early columns.

In fact, in the summer of 2001, with the goal of learning more about the issue of sex abuse in the Church, the *Globe*'s Rezendes contacted Richard Sipe and had him flown to Boston.[2] It is hard to imagine the source of Sipe coming from anywhere but the *Phoenix*.

In the years after 2002, the *Phoenix* would often trumpet the fact that it was the first paper – and not the *Globe* – to report Boston's Catholic sex abuse story. A full-page ad promoting the *Phoenix* would display both the cover of the March 23, 2001, issue of the *Phoenix* (featuring Kristen Lombardi's first explosive piece) and that of the January 6, 2002, edition of the *Globe* (the first day of that paper's abuse series) with the words, "Some papers lead … Other papers follow." (Similarly, ads promoting the *Phoenix* on local radio station WFNX (which was owned by the *Phoenix* from 1983 to 2012) also frequently reminded listeners which paper had first launched the story.)

Years later, *Phoenix* publisher Stephen Mindich would praise the *Globe*'s coverage of the scandals as "amazing" and "remarkable," but he would add:

> "[T]hey didn't give us the credit at the time that we deserve … [T]hey weren't there. They didn't do the story. They didn't break the story."[3]

Indeed, neither the name Kristen Lombardi nor the *Boston Phoenix* appear in any of the 989 Catholic abuse items that the *Globe* published in its celebrated coverage in 2002.

NOTES

1 Kristen Lombardi, "Cardinal Sin: Cardinal Law, the Church, and Pedophilia," *Boston Phoenix*, March 23, 2001. By "not completely accurate," we point to a fact that the *Phoenix* admitted that it misquoted a lawyer featured in Lombardi's piece: "Letters to the editor," *Boston Phoenix*, April 12, 2001. ("We were mistaken when we said [lawyer Stephen J.] Lyons was in possession of evidence implicating the Cardinal, but which he could not reveal due to confidentiality orders.")

2 Michael D'Antonio (2003). *Mortal sins: Sex, crime, and the era of Catholic scandal* (New York: Thomas Dunne Press, St. Martin's Press), p. 246.

3 Interview with Stephen Mindich, August 6, 2012, edition of *Greater Boston* (TV show), host Emily Rooney, WGBH-TV. Mindich would also add, "I don't know if [the *Globe*] would have the resources today to do [the abuse story]."

It wasn't the *Globe*!

In the years after 2002, Boston's weekly arts newspaper the Boston Phoenix *often reminded readers with a full-page ad that it actually reported the Catholic Church sex abuse story in Boston almost a whole year before the* Globe *did.*

19

Sickness Unleashed

The name of John J. Geoghan has become synonymous with the Catholic sex abuse scandal in Boston.

Born in 1931, raised in the Boston neighborhood of West Roxbury, and ordained as a priest from Boston's St. John's Seminary in 1962, Geoghan quite simply never should have become a Catholic priest to begin with.

Even in his early days of priestly training, there were signs that Geoghan did not have the maturity, intelligence, and resiliency for the priesthood. Geoghan was already known for suffering from a "nervous condition" and depression, and after a few years of seminary, he was said to be "sick," "unhappy," and "wrestling with his soul."[1]

"Scholastically he is a problem," a seminary rector noted, while teaching staff could not help but indicate that Geoghan was "feminine in his manner and speech."[2]

Ironically, while Geoghan would later torch the innocent lives of scores of young boys, his first year of his priesthood was marked by a news-making episode in which he actually saved a desperate man's life. Driving home over Boston's Mystic River Bridge[3] on Christmas afternoon in 1962,

Geoghan spotted a suicidal man contemplating a leap. The young priest talked and pleaded with the man for 15 minutes before he agreed to come down into the safety of the hands of Boston police and firemen.[4]

Yet it was learned decades later that Geoghan had already been molesting boys in his first assignment that year, Blessed Sacrament Parish in Saugus. In 1995, the Archdiocese of Boston paid out financial settlements on claims that while in Saugus the sick Geoghan molested four boys in the same family.[5]

Although Geoghan undoubtedly molested boys in the 1960s and 1970s, the first actual record of an accusation of abuse by Geoghan in an archdiocesan file appears to be in 1979. At the time, the leader of the Archdiocese of Boston was Cardinal Humberto Medeiros, and the action that the archdiocese took in late 1979 was typical for its era. The Church placed Geoghan on "sick leave," keeping him out of ministry for a full, entire year – from early 1980 to early 1981, not a short period of time – and had him undergo psychiatric "treatment." It also sent Geoghan on a sabbatical to Rome.

Yet over the next several years, a pattern repeated itself tragically:

- Geoghan abused;
- The Church removed him from his assignment;
- The Church sent him to "treatment," and therapists would recommend his return to ministry; and
- The Church placed him in a new parish.

In July of 2001, about a half-year before the *Globe* began its full-on blitzkrieg against the Church, lawsuits against the Archdiocese of Boston involving its handling of Geoghan were regularly in the news. Wilson D. Rogers, Jr., chief counsel to the archdiocese, felt compelled to respond to what he felt were unfair attacks against the archdiocese in the media.

In a front-page letter in *The Pilot*, the archdiocesan weekly newspaper, Rogers directly replied to a claim in the media by a Church-suing lawyer about how the Church handled the case of John Geoghan:

> "[The lawyer] has never once mentioned that each assignment of John Geoghan, subsequent to the first complaint of sexual misconduct, was incident to an independent medical evaluation advising that such assignment was appropriate and safe."[6]

In fact, Rogers' claim is unquestionably true. And this important aspect was very much the most downplayed element in all of the *Globe*'s reporting of the entire Geoghan narrative.

In 1981, after Geoghan had been out of ministry and in "treatment" for a full year, Boston's Dr. John H. Brennan, M.D, one of two doctors treating Geoghan, wrote that it was "mutually agreed that he was now able to resume his priestly duties."[7]

Three years later, in 1984, the Church removed Geoghan after yet more complaints. However, in December 1984, Dr. Brennan wrote that Geoghan "has been under my care for the past seven years" and that "there are no psychiatric contraindications or restrictions to his work as a parish priest."[8] A second doctor who treated Geoghan, Robert W. Mullins, M.D., wrote that Geoghan has "adjusted remarkedly [*sic*] well" to treatment following his recent removal, and added, "In my opinion, he is now able to resume full Pastoral [*sic*] activities without need for any specific restrictions."[9]

In its 2002 coverage, the *Globe* would challenge the professional qualifications of Brennan and Mullins to treat Geoghan and make such recommendations.[10] But the paper could not say the same for the professional doctors who treated Geoghan in 1989 and *were* professionally qualified to assess the perverted cleric.

In March 1989, after the archdiocese learned of new accusations against Geoghan, it sent Geoghan to the St. Luke Institute in Maryland, the very treatment center operated by Rev. Michael Peterson, one of the co-authors of a 1985 clergy sex abuse report to bishops about how the Church should deal with abusive priests. (See much more about the 1985 report in Chapter 22.)

In other words, Cardinal Law explicitly followed the exact advice given to him in 1985. Law sent Geoghan into the hands of the so-called "experts" who claimed to have the "answers" to the Church's abuse problem.

After assessing Geoghan for a week-and-a-half, St. Luke Institute determined Geoghan was a "homosexual pedophile" and referred him to the Institute for Living, another treatment center in Hartford, Connecticut, which was considered the most prestigious of such centers in the country. While being examined by a team of secular psychologists, Geoghan would reside there for nearly three months beginning in August 1989.

In November of 1989, the Institute conveyed reports that appeared to stun even Church officials. While declaring that Geoghan harbored the diagnosis of "atypical pedophilia, in remission," psychologists at the esteemed Institute stated that Geoghan was "moderately improved" and fit for pastoral ministry and would not pose a danger to churchgoers.

Following the Institute's recommendations, Msgr. Robert

J. Banks, the Vicar for Administration for the Archdiocese, actually wrote back to doctors asking for clarification of their findings. Concerned about the basis for the psychologists' judgments, Banks specifically wrote of the worry that Geoghan "would not present a risk for the parishioners he would serve."[11]

Within days, a doctor at The Institute of Living, Dr. Robert F. Swords, M.D., wrote back to Msgr. Banks:

> "We judge Father Geoghan to be **clinically quite safe** to resume his pastoral ministry after observation, evaluation, and treatment here for three months. The probability that he would sexually act out again is quite low … It is both **reasonable and therapeutic** for him to be reassigned back to his parish" (bold added).[12]

And a year later, in December 1990, Dr. Swords penned a *second* letter in which he stated that Geoghan was "fit for pastoral work in general **including children**."[13]

Yet never once in the several dozen articles that the *Globe* published about the long story of John Geoghan did the paper ever quote the line from Dr. Swords that he believed it was "reasonable and therapeutic" for the Church to return Geoghan to a parish. Not once. Surely this omission by the *Globe* was not an accident.

Geoghan was a priest who already had a horrific record of molesting boys for over a quarter century, yet a team of secular psychologists determined that it was "clinically quite safe" as well as "reasonable and therapeutic" to work in a parish, *even with children.*

For many years before 2002, Cardinal Law and other bishops were repeatedly advised that abusive priests should immediately be put under the care of psychologists. (Read *much* more about this in Chapter 22.) Doctors adamantly asserted that "treatment can help rehabilitate clerics so that they may return to active ministry in most instances."[14]

Decades later, we now know that the number one mistake that Cardinal Law and the leaders in Boston made in the entire scandals was trusting secular psychologists who had the Church and all of society believe that abusive pedophiles could somehow be "rehabilitated" and successfully return to work with access to children.

[Essential question: Why should Cardinal Law be bludgeoned in the media for following the advice of professional psychologists decades ago but current-day Church leaders (like Law's successor, Cardinal Seán O'Malley) be *praised* for adhering to the instruction from the *very same* field of psychologists *today*?]

NOTES

1 The Investigative Staff of The Boston Globe, *Betrayal: The Crisis in the Catholic Church* (Boston: Little, Brown and Company, 2002), p.16, 17.

2 *Betrayal*, p. 15.

3 The Mystic River Bridge is now known today as the Tobin Bridge.

4 "Saugus curate foils leap off Mystic Bridge," *The Boston Globe*, December 26, 1962, p.1 (photo on page 11.) [Note: Geoghan's name is misspelled in the article as "Geoughan."]

5 *Betrayal*, p. 18.

6 Boston Pilot, July, 2001, p. 1.

7 Dr. Brennan to Bishop Thomas V. Daily, letter dated January 13, 1981.

8 Dr. Brennan to Rev. Robert J. Banks, letter dated December 14, 1984.

[9] Dr. Robert W. Mullins, M.D., to Rev. Thomas F. Oates, October 1984.
[10] Michael Rezendes and Matt Carroll, "Doctors who OK'd Geoghan lacked expertise, review shows," *The Boston Globe*, January 16, 2002.
[11] Msgr. Robert J. Banks to Dr. Vincent J. Stephens, M.D., The Institute of Living, letter dated November 30, 1989. Note: A January 24, 2002, article in the *Globe* would darkly suggest that Banks' letter to the Institute "sought … a more favorable diagnosis" for Geoghan. But this is a gross, if not flat-out dishonest, misrepresentation of Banks' letter.
[12] Dr. Robert F. Swords, M.D., The Institute of Living, to Msgr. Banks, letter dated December 13, 1989.
[13] Dr. Robert F. Swords, M.D., The Institute of Living, to Msgr. Banks, letter December 1990, cited in Michael Rezendes, "Memos offer split view of priest," *The Boston Globe*, January 24, 2002, p. A1.
[14] Rev. Michael R. Peterson, M.D., "Guidelines," December 9, 1985.

20

Doctors and Letters

In the *Globe*'s relentless reporting on the case of pedophile John Geoghan, a humongous, front-page article on January 24, 2002, is notable for a number of flat-out falsehoods and misleading information.

In the column, the *Globe*'s Walter Robinson and Matt Carroll reported on a letter dated September 6, 1984 – just six months after Law was officially installed in Boston – written by a woman named Margaret Gallant from the nearby suburb of Stoughton and addressed to then-Archbishop Law.

Gallant wrote to Law with her concern that Fr. Geoghan had been assigned to a family parish in Dorchester, a neighborhood of Boston, in light of the fact that Geoghan "has been known in the past to molest boys," including a number from her extended family.

Writing with a devotion to the Church that was clearly palpable, Gallant expressed her profound fear that Geoghan was still in ministry. Having also written to Law's predecessor, Cardinal Medeiros, two years earlier, Gallant reiterated her "very real fear of the disgrace this would bring to the church, to all good priests and families, and finally, but most importantly, my fellow members in this Body of Christ who are left in the dark as to the danger their children are in, while I have knowledge of the truth."[1]

Robinson and Carroll trumpeted Gallant's letter as additional proof that Law "ignored" warnings about Geoghan and somehow "supported" the priest in his terror of abuse.[2] And in case readers were not convinced of the portrayal of callousness that they were trying to construct of Cardinal Law, the pair added the claim:

> "The records do not contain any evidence that Law replied to Gallant."[3]

In truth, Cardinal Law *did* indeed reply to Ms. Gallant, as anyone can plainly see. (See page 107.)

In his letter, Cardinal Law thanked Ms. Gallant for her letter and informed her that her "concern [was] being investigated."[4] Robinson and Carroll were just flat-out wrong.

But that's not all. Robinson and Carroll also claimed in the article that Gallant had written her letter to Law after Law had already removed Geoghan from his Dorchester assignment. In fact, dated letters in Geoghan's file actually show that days after receiving the emotional letter from Ms. Gallant, Cardinal Law stripped Geoghan from the Dorchester parish, and handwritten notes in Geoghan's file explicitly cite Gallant's letter as an impetus for doing so.[5]

Again, Robinson's and Carroll's reporting was clearly erroneous.[6]

Tragically, Cardinal Law relied on the same practice of not only his predecessor but that of society at large. Law and the Church entrusted the criminal Geoghan to the care of two different Boston-area psychologists. And within weeks, both men asserted that Geoghan was somehow fit to return to ministry. Dr. Robert W. Mullins, M.D., not only claimed that Geoghan was "now able to resume full pastoral ministry, without any specific restrictions,"[7] but that Geoghan was "fully recovered."[8] Meanwhile, Dr. John H. Brennan, M.D., wrote that there were "no psychiatric contraindications or restrictions to his work as a parish priest."[9]

On the recommendation he received from the so-called "experts," Cardinal Law appointed Geoghan to St. Julia Parish in the tony Boston suburb of Weston.

And in the very same article by Robinson and Carroll, the *Globe* also misrepresented a December 7, 1984, letter to then-Archbishop Law written by Bishop John M. D'Arcy, who expressed concerns about the assignment of Geoghan to St. Julia's in light of Geoghan's "homosexual involvement with young boys."

The *Globe* trumpeted the letter as more evidence that the Church "repeatedly ignored" warnings about Geoghan. But the *Globe* conveniently left out some important aspects of D'Arcy's letter.

When one actually reads Bishop D'Arcy's letter, it is clear that his overriding concern was that St. Julia's was a "troubled and divided parish" and there was "great animosity" towards the long-standing pastor there (Msgr. Francis S. Rossiter). "The complaints center around [Rossiter's] style and manner that is perceived by many to be overbearing and authoritarian," D'Arcy wrote.

Although the *Globe* would have had readers believe otherwise – and this is important – D'Arcy never actually recommended or suggested in his letter that Geoghan not serve at St. Julia's. In fact, Bishop D'Arcy proposed the *opposite*: that Geoghan *not* be removed from St. Julia's, lest parishioners "quickly claim that once again that Monsignor

Rossiter cannot live with other priests."

"I wonder if Fr. Geoghan should be reduced to just weekend work while receiving some kind of therapy," D'Arcy offered.[10]

And, in truth, D'Arcy's suggestion that Geoghan receive "some kind of therapy" was already being implemented. And since such a measure would have been a private, personnel matter, D'Arcy likely would not have been even aware of it.

So, in a nutshell, rather than buttressing the argument that the Church "ignored" and "supported" Geoghan, D'Arcy's letter only underscores the undeniable fact that the prevailing belief at the time – not just in the Church, but also in society at large – was that "therapy" could somehow successfully manage the warped behavior of ill individuals like Geoghan.

(Ironically, in an October 2002 deposition about how he handled the case of John Geoghan, Cardinal Law testified that he actually garnered a "great deal of criticism" from parishioners at St. Julia's for removing the abusive priest. Geoghan was reportedly popular there, and the vast majority of parishioners were completely unaware of his crimes.[11])

The *Globe* is just plain wrong

September 21, 1984

Mrs. Marge Gallant
346 Walnut Street
Stoughton
MA 02072

Dear Mrs. Gallant:

Thank you for your letter of September 6, 1984 concerning the priest at St. Brendan's, Dorchester.

The matter of your concern is being investigated and appropriate pastoral decisions will be made both for the priest and God's people.

Thank you for your concern. Please pray for me.

With warm personal regards, I am

Sincerely yours in Christ,

Archbishop of Boston

On January 24, 2002, the Globe*'s Walter V. Robinson and Matt Carroll reported that "the records do not contain any evidence" that Cardinal Law responded to a complaint from resident Marge Gallant about abuse by then-priest John Geoghan. This letter clearly proves otherwise. In fact, contrary to the* Globe*'s reporting, Cardinal Law removed Geoghan from his parish assignment almost immediately after receiving the complaint from Gallant.*

NOTES

1 Margaret Gallant to Cardinal Law, letter dated September 6, 1984.

---

[2] Michael Rezendes and The Spotlight Team, "Church allowed abuse by priest for years," *The Boston Globe*, January 6, 2002.
[3] Walter V. Robinson and Matt Carroll, "Documents show church long supported Geoghan," *The Boston Globe*, January 24, 2002.
[4] Cardinal Law to Marge Gallant, letter dated September 21, 1984. [Note: Some have cited the "impersonal" tone in Law's response to Gallant, but Cardinal Law was certainly not at liberty to provide confidential personnel history and medical information to a private citizen.]
[5] Bishop Robert J. Banks handwritten notes dated September 17, 1984.
[6] The next day, the *Globe*'s Sacha Pfeiffer corrected the record regarding Law's letter to Gallant. However, whereas Robinson's and Carroll's article ran nearly 2,500 words on page 1, the *Globe*'s de facto correction from Pfeiffer ran a modest 325 words and was buried on page 21.
[7] Dr. Robert W. Mullins to Rev. Thomas F. Oates, letter dated October 20, 1984.
[8] "Summary of allegations" by Rev. Brian M. Flatley, memo dated July 11, 1996.
[9] Dr. John H. Brennan to Rev. Robert J. Banks, letter dated December 14, 1984.
[10] Bishop John M. D'Arcy to Archbishop Bernard F. Law, letter dated December 7, 1984.
[11] Deposition of Cardinal Bernard Law, October 11, 2002, Offices of Greenberg Traurig, Boston, deposed by Boston lawyer Roderick MacLeish Jr.

21

The Police Knew – in 1979!

In its tsunami of reporting against the Catholic Church, the *Boston Globe* underreported and misled its readers about another tragic element of the Geoghan narrative.

In truth, many years before Geoghan exited the priesthood, Boston police could have put an end to Geoghan's abominable spree of abuse, but it didn't.

In its January 2002 coverage, the *Globe* published an article by Stephen Kurkjian and Sacha Pfeiffer, "Police probed [Geoghan] on sex abuse as early as 1986."[1] Yet this headline was completely false. In fact, Geoghan's personnel file contains at least two letters that show that Boston Police actually knew about accusations against Geoghan many years earlier – in *1979*.[2]

Tragically, in light of what was happening in the Boston area in 1979 with child molestation cases (see Chapter 10), it is almost easy to see how police felt no urgency to put a halt to Geoghan's sick activities. Judges were simply slapping sodomizers of young boys with probation, and investigations into gay child sex abuse were being loudly denounced in the media as "witch hunts." Therefore, it is no surprise that police did not expend much of an effort to stop the criminal

Geoghan.

Yet in all of the *Globe*'s reporting, there is no mention at all that police knew about Geoghan as early as 1979.

And the *Globe* also obfuscated another important fact about why police never prosecuted Geoghan in the 1980s when it had the chance. Buried at the end of their article, Kurkjian and Pfeiffer wrote, "[P]olice decided not to go forward with prosecution because the parents of the victims said they would not cooperate."[3]

This is a crucial fact. Police cannot move forward and prosecute cases without cooperating witnesses. Indeed, it was not until *1999*, already after Geoghan was removed from the priesthood, that police secured the witnesses it needed to prosecute the criminal ex-priest.

"Old news" by January 2002?

While many have been under the impression that it was the *Boston Globe* who first uncovered the crimes of the notorious John Geoghan in January of 2002, the truth is that John Geoghan was already nearly a household name in the Boston area by that time to anyone who read the newspaper or watched television regularly.

News of Geoghan's reign of abuse first became public in 1996, *six years* before the *Globe*'s 2002 coverage, when a number of people came forward with lawsuits claiming that Geoghan had abused them years earlier, and it was widely reported that he had indeed abused many children dating back to the 1960s.

Geoghan's name would repeatedly resurface in the media, such as in 1997, when Cardinal Law and the Archdiocese of

Boston publicly announced the first of a series of "Healing Masses" to reach out to victims of priest sex abuse. Surely the news of Geoghan's egregious crimes had been an impetus for such a measure.

And when the archdiocese announced in June of 1998 that the Church had "defrocked" Geoghan from the priesthood for repeated acts of sex abuse against children, it was the *lead story* on all four Boston-area television newscasts that evening. It was also front-page news in newspapers all across New England, including, of course, the *Boston Globe.* In fact, the *Globe* was already asserting that the high-profile Geoghan case "has been a public relations nightmare for the Archdiocese of Boston."[4]

In 1999, when law enforcement arraigned John Geoghan, it was a major story as well, as television cameras and journalists swarmed both the Middlesex and Suffolk County courthouses.

Lawsuits and criminal charges involving Geoghan continued to snowball in 2000 and 2001, and those stories received wide media attention as well.

In the end, long before January 6, 2002, when the *Boston Globe* began its blitzkrieg of stories of abuse in the Catholic Church, the sad and maddening Geoghan case was already a well-known story. The paper had already published *over three dozen items* about the abuse by John Geoghan.

NOTES

[1] Stephen Kurkjian and Sacha Pfeiffer, "Police probed priest on sex abuse as early as 1986," *The Boston Globe*, January 25, 2002, p. A21.

[2] Letter from Fr. Frank Delaney to Bishop Thomas V. Daily, August 17, 1979 and letter from Bishop Thomas V. Daily to Fr. Frank Delaney (reporting he spoke to a chaplain at the Boston Police), August 23, 1979.

[3] Kurkjian and Pfeiffer.

[4] Diego Ribadeneira, "Cardinal announces defrocking of priest," *The Boston Globe*, June 7, 1998, p. A1.

22

That 1985 Report

Early in its 2002 coverage, the *Boston Globe* prominently cited an important report that had been written back in 1985 by a trio of men that foresaw the scope of the crisis that the Catholic Church was facing regarding abuse by priests.

The 1985 report, entitled "The Problem of Sexual Molestation by Roman Catholic Clergy: Meeting the Problem in a Comprehensive and Responsible Manner," was written on the heels of the first nationally renowned story of sex abuse by a Catholic priest, the notorious case of Gilbert Gauthe in Louisiana.

Three men authored the report:

- Rev. Thomas P. Doyle, a Dominican priest and canon lawyer;

- F. Ray Mouton, Jr., a lawyer, who in the mid-1980s had defended Gauthe; and

- Rev. Michael R. Peterson, a priest-psychologist who had founded St. Luke Institute, a psychiatric hospital in Silver Spring Maryland, which often treated abusive clergy.

The trio convened to write the report to address what they rightly believed to be a glaring and growing problem in the Church. (Astonishingly, Rev. Doyle has openly admitted that Cardinal Law was "very supportive" and an early ally of the group's report.[1])

What did the 1985 report say? For starters, the report correctly noted that the Church was facing a major crisis. Catholic priests had abused children, and there was colossal harm being wreaked upon victims as well as the Church.

The 92-page report also aptly observed that American society had transformed in its litigiousness in recent years. Whereas there was once a time that suing a doctor was unthinkable, malpractice lawsuits had now become commonplace. This change in the culture had serious implications for the Catholic Church, the report correctly indicated. The trio also accurately noted that contingency lawyers clearly had the Catholic Church in their crosshairs.

However, most of the report was spent outlining a number of steps which bishops and the Church should take in dealing with abusive priests on both the pastoral and legal levels.

Most notably, the trio wholeheartedly believed that priests who abused children could return to active ministry following psychological treatment.

In a supplemental chapter to the trio's 1985 report, Rev. Peterson would write, "These are lifelong diseases for which there is now *much hope for recovery and control of the disorders*" (italics added).

That's right. The authors of the 1985 actually believed, as almost all psychologists did at the time, that there could be "recovery and control" for abusive pedophiles.

Peterson also added (emphasis added):

"**It is a fact** that treatment can help rehabilitate clerics so that they may return to active ministry in most instances irregardless [*sic*] of jail time or no legal complications."[2]

It's true. Peterson clearly believed and advocated that priests who abused kids, if properly "treated," could most certainly return to active ministry, even if they have served time in prison or been sued!

Yet years later in 2002, the *Globe* deceived its readers by grossly misrepresenting and manipulating the contents of the report.

On only the second day of the paper's 2002 coverage, January 7, the *Globe*'s Michael Rezendes essentially left his readers with the impression that the 1985 report had conveyed to Cardinal Law and other bishops that it would be reckless to ever return abusive priests to active ministry.[3]

At the beginning of his article, Rezendes emphatically quoted from the 1985 report at the beginning of his article:

> "Recidivism is so high with pedophilia ... that all controlled studies have shown that traditional outpatient psychiatric or psychological models alone do not work."[4]

For Rezendes, this quotation from the report was the equivalent of a "smoking gun." And in subsequent weeks, in addition to other colleagues at the *Globe*, other newspapers, including the *New York Times* and the *Baltimore Sun*, would use Rezendes' citation as a way to plaster Cardinal Law.[5] Even a number of reputable Catholic writers would find Rezendes' citation useful.

However, these other media outlets were completely oblivious to the fact that Rezendes' quote was completely deceptive.

While Rezendes gave readers the impression that the report concluded that treatment of abusive priests was futile and that such priests should never be returned to ministry, we know that the exact *opposite* was the case. The trio's report strongly recommended psychological treatment as a first course of action as soon as a priest was found to have abused a minor.

When Rezendes artfully cited the line that "traditional outpatient psychiatric or psychological models alone do not work" with pedophiles, the key words in the citation are "*outpatient*" and "*traditional.*"

The report was asserting that priests could not simply make routine *outpatient* visits to a psychologist, which had *traditionally* been the case. Instead, the report recommended a more comprehensive, "family model" approach to treatment which involved months-long *inpatient* therapies.

The report explained that in addition to professional management, "This means that members of the religious family involved with the priest prior to treatment should be involved in the treatment and in the post treatment plans."[6]

Yet this important aspect of the report's recommendations was deftly omitted by Rezendes and the *Globe*. Rezendes craftily cherry-picked a quote to give readers the impression that the report was alerting bishops that psychological treatment of abusive priests was futile, when the truth was something entirely different.

See the deception?

The bottom line: the *Boston Globe* would have you believe that if Church leaders had followed the advice of a report back in 1985 written by a trio of guys who understood the scope of the problem, a major crisis could have been averted.

The implication from the *Globe* was that Cardinal Law and other American bishops somehow "ignored" the 1985 report.[7]

But the fact is that too many bishops, including Cardinal Law, *did* follow the advice from the report that Doyle, Peterson, and Mouton gave to them in 1985. Church officials routinely sent abusive priests off to treatment facilities where professional psychologists would later claim that the clerics were fit to return to ministry.

The results of this common practice, perhaps no better illustrated than in the maddening case of John Geoghan, were *disastrous.*

NOTES

1 Kristen Lombardi, "Failure to Act," *The Boston Phoenix*, October 4, 2001.
2 Rev. Michael R. Peterson, M.D., "Guidelines," December 9, 1985.
3 Michael Rezendes, "In 1985, Law had report on repeat abusers," *The Boston Globe*, January 7, 2002, p. A12. [Important note: It should be noted that the "recidivism" quotation that Rezendes cited were nowhere in the 92 pages of the 1985 report written by the trio. Nowhere. In truth, Rezendes was citing a supplemental paper by Rev. Peterson written months after the original 92-page report.]
4 Michael R. Peterson, President/Executive Medical Director, St. Luke Institute, "Guidelines: With Materials by Berlin, Doyle, Mouton, and Others," December 9, 1985.
5 See: Derrick Z. Jackson, "Why won't Law back disclosing past sex abuse?" *The Boston Globe*, January 18, 2002, p. A23.; R. Scott Appleby, "'Betrayal': Covering the Church Crisis," *The New York Times*, July 14, 2002; Gail Gibson and John Rivera, "Maryland center claims success treating priests," *The Baltimore Sun*, April 11, 2002.
6 Rev. Michael R. Peterson, M.D.; Rev. Thomas P. Doyle, J.C.D;

F. Ray Mouton, Esq., "The Problem of Sexual Molestation by Roman Catholic Clergy: Meeting the Problem in a Comprehensive and Responsible Manner," June 1985, p. 56.

[7] It is true that bishops did not follow a piece of advice from the report that a national "Crisis Control Team" be formed to work with bishops and priests on the sex abuse issue. Bishops felt that abuse cases would be best handled on a local, diocesan level. However, it is unclear at best how the formation of such a committee would have been able to stem the avalanche of lawsuits against the Church in subsequent years.

23

Globe Sources

Any veteran journalist knows that a good story needs good sources to support that story. And when the *Boston Globe* needed sources to blast away at the Catholic Church over the sex abuse issue, the paper turned to a number of reliable voices who could fulfill the role just as the paper wanted.

One frequent source often seen in the *Globe*'s coverage was Rev. Thomas P. Doyle, O.P., a Dominican priest and canon lawyer. What the *Globe* has never told readers, however, is of Doyle's storied history of contempt for the Church and a penchant to misrepresent the faith. Doyle's open disdain for the Catholic Church is so exaggerated and over the top, one cannot help but wonder why he still remains a Catholic priest.

Globe writers never once mentioned Doyle's very lengthy record of dissent and animosity against the Catholic Church. For example, when addressing an audience in Chicago in 2012, Doyle essentially conceded that he is barely even Catholic by declaring that while he is "still legally a priest," he freely acknowledged that he has "nothing to do with the Catholic Church," he has "nothing to do with the clerical life," he is "not associated with the Church in any way," he operates on his own, and his beliefs are "about as far away from the Vatican as you can get."[1] In addition, in the past, Doyle:

- has dismissed Catholic thought as "childish, unrealistic beliefs" and "magical thinking"[2];
- has likened the Catholic Church to the Nazi party by writing "the [Catholic] hierarchy is about the most corrupt political entity on the globe. At least with the Nazis you knew what you were dealing with"[3];
- has been banned from acting as a canon lawyer in the Archdiocese of St. Louis for committing serious canonical crimes[4];
- has been formally reprimanded as a military chaplain after he was arrested for drunk driving[5];
- has demeaned priestly vestments as "dresses"[6];
- has wildly claimed in a 2012 commentary that "Nothing has changed since 1985" in the Church's handling of abuse cases[7]; and
- has stated in a 2010 television interview that the Catholic Church "ought to sell the Vatican to the Mormons or to Disney or something, and go out and start all over again."[8]

Doyle has also been a close cohort and ally of the anti-Catholic group SNAP (Survivors Network of those Abused by Priests), often appearing as a speaker at their annual conferences. In July 2007, the group even awarded Doyle its "Red Badge of Courage" award.[9]

In other words, Fr. Doyle most certainly has never provided a reliable representation of the Catholic faith and the Catholic Church abuse narrative. As an angry leftist and dissident, Doyle was hardly the unbiased "expert" that the *Globe* purported him to be.

Another favorite source for the *Globe* was Richard Sipe, an 80-year-old ex-priest and mental health counselor.

Just as with Fr. Doyle, the *Globe* never told readers of Sipe's troubling track record of falsehoods, distortions, and nastiness. As is frequently the case with other purported experts cited by the media, Sipe uses the issue of clergy sex abuse as a means to advance his attack on the Catholic Church, especially its teachings regarding human sexuality.

To understand how disdainful Sipe can be of the Church and its teachings, especially those related to sexuality and priest celibacy, one can simply look to his 1995 book, *Sex, Priests, And Power: Anatomy Of A Crisis.*

In his book, Sipe actually claims the Church's so-called "celibate/sexual power system" was a root cause of the Nazi Holocaust. One must read it to believe it:

> "The most frightening aspect of analyzing the structure of the celibate/sexual power system is to realize how it was determined by banal sexual impulses which women are the objects of domination …
>
> "When I substitute 'Jew' or 'homosexual' for 'woman' in the schema, I am struck with how everything fits with Nazi theory and practice … Numerous parallels with the celibate/sexual power system make it chillingly familiar and force us to acknowledge that they both, system and power, spring from the same human impulses. I cannot forget that the people and forces that generated Nazism and the Holocaust were all products of one Christian culture and the celibate/sexual power system." (pp. 179-

180)[10]

However, Sipe's wild theories about the Holocaust should not be a surprise considering some other public statements that the bitter ex-priest has made. In a 2010 feature about Pope Benedict, Sipe actually claimed to ABC News that "several hundred [popes] have been murdered" in the Catholic Church's 2000-year history.[11]

It is a bizarre assertion, indeed, considering the fact that there have only been about 266 popes since the Catholic Church's foundation.

Sipe's frequent media appearances are rife with inflammatory rhetoric that neither advances the discussion about protecting children from abuse nor provides any concrete support for past victims.

For example, in a 2013 appearance in an HBO documentary *Mea Maxima Culpa: Silence in the House of God*, Sipe claimed he has "great respect" for the Catholic Church, but then in the very next breath he actually asserted that the Church knowingly and intentionally "selects, cultivates, protects, defends, and produces sexual abusers."[12]

One wonders who on earth could possibly "respect" an organization that would target children to be used as sex objects. Yet Sipe appears to want to give off an air of credibility by claiming "respect" for the Church so he can advance his wild theories and claims about the Catholic Church and its teachings.

Influence from gay activists at the *Globe*?

In an article on November 3, 1997, the *Boston Globe*'s Jack Thomas, the paper's "ombudsman" at the time, openly admitted that the *Globe* employed two "gay activists" as copy editors at the paper.

One of the activists was Peter Accardi, who worked at the Globe for 42 years until his retirement in 2007. The other was Robert Hardman, who was also a majority owner of *Out* magazine, a popular monthly publication aimed at the gay community. After investing $4 million into the magazine in the early 1990s,[13] Hardman sold his share in 2000 to a rival publication.

What role did these men play in the editorial decisions at the paper? Well, in October of 1997, Jeff Jacoby, the lone conservative columnist at the *Globe*, wrote an opinion article called, "Where's the tolerance now?"

In the column Jacoby took issue with gay activists at nearby Harvard University who had recently destroyed signs made by a Christian group at Harvard promoting an event which featured a speaker who had denounced his former gay lifestyle.

The activists also mocked that anyone who belonged to this Christian group as being a Nazi.[14] In response to this, Jacoby wrote:

"[I]n bastions of the left from Harvard to Hollywood, it is routine. Dare to suggest that homosexuality may not be something to celebrate, and instantly you are a Nazi, a hatemonger, a gas-chamber operator. Offer to share your teachings of Christianity or Judaism with students 'struggling with homosexuality,' and you become as vile as a Ku Kluxer, as despicable as David Duke …

"How was inviting this man to speak at Harvard analogous to sending Jews to gas chambers? Isn't his experience also an element of human 'diversity'? What does it say about gay advocates, who so loudly champion tolerance and freedom of sexual choice, that they are so poisonously intolerant of people who make a choice different from theirs?"

For Jacoby merely expressing this opinion, it was reported that the *Globe*'s Accardi and Hardiman (the two gay activist copy editors) were "incensed" and loudly complained to their higher-ups.[15]

The *Globe* ombudsman Thomas responded with a column a short time later in which he outright slammed Jacoby for being "often intolerant," "frequently overbearing," and "sometimes downright insulting."[16]

Although Jacoby had expressed an opinion that was entirely consistent with Judeo-Christian thinking for over two millennia, Thomas asserted that Jacoby's column was a "a high price to pay for freedom of the press" and that Jacoby's future articles dealing with homosexuality "will be judged case by case."

To this, Jacoby responded, "I can assure you that on no topic – not race, not the death penalty, not multiculturalism, not welfare – are you made to endure as much fury as you have to endure if you say anything on this topic [homosexuality] that is considered politically incorrect."[17]

So by the late 1990s, an editorial policy was crystal clear at the *Globe*: You can belittle, smear, and insult Catholics, but you cannot say anything that might be just a bit unflattering to homosexuals.

NOTES

1 "SNAP CONFERENCE 2012 EXCLUSIVE: Dissident Priest Doyle Trashes Bishops and Admits He Has 'Nothing To Do With the Catholic Church'," TheMediaReport.com, August 14, 2002.
2 Thomas P. Doyle, J.C.D., C.A.D.C., "A revised version of an address given on July 22, 2006, SNAP National Conference, Jersey City, New Jersey," posted at http://arcc-catholic-rights.net/. (Accessed January 2015)
3 The quote originally appeared in a private email that appeared on the web site www.theinquiry.ca. The email is no longer there (as of January 2015, at least), but Doyle acknowledged in a court declaration on June 1, 2012, "a comparison I made between the Catholic bishops and Nazis (not an analogy to Nazism)." See "Declaration of Thomas P. Doyle," Case 3:02-cv-00430-MO, Document 326, Filed June 1, 2012, page 10.
4 "DECREE EXTRA-JUDICIAL ADJUDICATION In the Matter of the Rev. [Thomas] Patrick Michael Doyle, O.P., J.C.D.," Archdiocese of St. Louis, April 9, 2008.
5 Michael D'Antonio (2003). *Mortal sins: Sex, crime, and the era of Catholic scandal* (New York: Thomas Dunne Press, St. Martin's Press), pp. 171-172.
6 William A. Donohue, "SNAP EXPOSED: Unmasking the Survivors Network of those Abused by Priests," a special report from the Catholic League for Religious and Civil Rights, August 22, 2011.
7 *Deliver Us from Evil*, 2006 film, directed by Amy Berg, Disarming Films.
8 *Dateline* (Australia TV show, SBS network), April 4, 2010 (Easter

Sunday!).

[9] There is a lot to say about SNAP (Survivors Network of those Abused by Priests). For more information, go to my site, TheMediaReport.com and click on the sidebar about SNAP.

[10] A.W. Richard Sipe (1995). *Sex, priests, and power: Anatomy of a crisis* (New York: Brunner/Mazel, Inc.), pp. 179-180.

[11] "Only God Can Fire Pope Benedict After Scandals" (page 2 of 2), abcnews.go.com, March 26, 2010.

[12] Quoted from *Mea Maxima Culpa: Silence in the House of God*, 2010 film, directed by Alex Gibney, Jigsaw Productions. Check out an extensive and lengthy rebuttal to *Mea Maxima Culpa* at TheMediaReport.com: "Hollywood vs. The Truth: HBO's New Anti-Catholic Documentary 'Mea Maxima Culpa: Silence in the House of God' EXPOSED"

[13] David W. Dunlap, "Out Magazine's Founder Resigns Amid Dispute," *The New York Times*, February 5, 1996.

[14] Jeff Jacoby, "Where's the tolerance now?" *The Boston Globe*, October 23, 1997, p. A25.

[15] Jack Thomas, "Should a column that targeted homosexuals have been published?" *The Boston Globe*, November 3, 1997, p. A15.

[16] Ibid.

[17] Ibid.

24

From *Globe* Celebrity to *Globe* Villain

Aside from John Geoghan, the most notorious name of an abusive priest in Boston may be that of Paul R. Shanley. Like his colleague John Geoghan, Shanley never should have been admitted to the priesthood, albeit for different reasons. Shanley was intelligent and engaging, and he related masterfully with marginalized youth and the gay community. However, Shanley openly dissented with the Church's teachings, in both speech and deed, especially on issues related to sexuality.

Shanley openly espoused that consensual sex between adults and teenage boys was permissible, if not beneficial, to both parties.[1] Even by his own admission, Shanley engaged in sexual activity with men, women, and teenage boys while a Catholic priest, admitting to sex acts with at least nine individuals during his priesthood,[2] although there may have been more. Once again, the harm inflicted upon his victims is unimaginable.

However, as with the case of Geoghan, the facts

surrounding the case of Paul Shanley were far more nuanced than those at the *Globe* would have had their readers believe.

Starting in the late 1960s, with the blessing of Boston's stalwart Cardinal Richard J. Cushing, Shanley built his reputation as a "street priest" who ministered to neglected and troubled youth in the rough-and-tumble areas of Boston. While Shanley often connected with runaways and other afflicted youth, he often aligned himself with Boston's vocal gay community. For several years, Shanley spearheaded an official diocesan ministry, the first of its kind in the country, specifically created to cater to Boston's gay Catholics.

Over time, Shanley became somewhat of a celebrity in the Boston area. And the one institution that did as much as anyone to celebrate and promote Shanley and his ministry was none other than the *Boston Globe.*

Starting in 1969 and continuing into the 1980s, the *Globe* published approximately *two dozen* different articles that cited Shanley and his work with Boston's gay and marginalized youth. In addition, Shanley often became a reliable source for the *Globe* when it needed a voice to bludgeon the Church over its teaching on homosexuality and its alleged "insensitivity" to homosexuals.[3]

By 2002, however, after spending years of building up Shanley as a pillar in the Boston community, the paper was probably hoping that readers had forgotten about the reams of glowing coverage that the paper had showered upon him decades earlier.

The case of Paul Shanley exploded on April 8, 2002 – during the zenith of the nationwide media coverage of the Catholic Church sex abuse story – when Church-suing attorney Roderick MacLeish, Jr. staged a press conference to unveil newly released personnel files concerning Shanley.

Seizing on the frenzied and over-the-top media coverage at the time, MacLeish did not just stage a press conference in a law office, where such events would normally have taken place. Instead, he reserved a large ballroom at the Sheraton Boston Hotel. An all-too-willing media packed the place, and MacLeish captured the opportunity to present old personnel documents about Shanley on a large projection screen behind him while lambasting Church officials. MacLeish also added a powerful emotional component to his presentation by showcasing his new clients who recently came forward to claim that they had been abused by the priest.

For a contingency lawyer who stood to score millions from suing the Church, MacLeish's media spectacle was quite a successful feat. Yet not a single one of the scores of media outlets, including the *Globe*, of course, bothered to question the motivations of MacLeish or challenge any of the rhetoric that MacLeish had unloaded at the press conference.

The very next day, April 9, 2002, the *Globe* ran *two* front-page stories about MacLeish's press event. (Notably, these two articles became the 65th and 66th Catholic sex abuse stories that the *Globe* had plastered on its front page since its coverage began only three months earlier. The paper's total number of abuse articles in a mere three months had already surpassed 240.)

The *Globe*'s articles contained a laundry list of accusations directed at Cardinal Law, charging that Law:

- promoted Shanley – "an alleged serial pedophile," according to the *Globe* – to pastor of a local church in 1984;
- gave him "a clean bill of health" to minister to Catholics in California; and
- "endorsed" him to lead a Catholic hostel in New

York.[4]

However, in the peak of this media tsunami of Catholic abuse stories, no one bothered to take a closer look at the facts.

In truth, although the *Globe* would have had their readers believe otherwise, in all the years that Cardinal Law and Rev. Shanley were in active ministry together in Boston, there was not a single written accusation of abuse made against Shanley at any time.[5] It was not until the fall of 1993 that Cardinal Law first became aware of the accusation that Shanley abused male teens decades earlier from the 1960s to the 1980s.

By 1993, however – and this is important to note – Shanley had already long been out of parish ministry in the Boston area. He was officially on sick leave, in ill health, and he was living in semi-retirement in Southern California. His role as a priest had been reduced to mere "weekend" work, filling in for unavailable priests at parishes in San Bernardino and Palm Springs when needed.[6]

And in October 1993, when a formal claim of abuse was filed regarding Shanley, Law immediately rescinded Shanley's permission to function in California and had him return to the East Coast, where he soon was sent to the Institute of Living treatment center in Connecticut.

And as far as the claim that Cardinal Law had "promoted" Shanley to be lead pastor at a suburban Boston parish back in December of 1984 (to be effective January 1, 1985), MacLeish, the *Globe*, and the rest of the media conveniently obfuscated the fact that Shanley had already been serving at that same parish for over four years. Law's predecessor, Cardinal Humberto Medeiros, had assigned Shanley there as associate pastor in 1979.

By November 1983, St. John's was without a pastor, so the archdiocesan Personnel Board appointed Shanley as the Parish Administrator, whose duties included, as his appointment letter stated at the time, "all financial matters, the administration of the rectory, all policy decisions, and all other matters pertaining to the pastoral care of the people of the parish." Shanley's assignment also included the directive that he "assume the obligation of the 'Missa pro populo' ['Mass for the People']."[7]

Law was not installed in Boston until months later, in March of 1984.

In other words, the so-called "promotion" of Shanley to lead pastor by Law was merely a formality to the actions that had already been implemented years earlier by Law's predecessors. With no complaints about Shanley in the nine months since he arrived in Boston, Law simply assumed that Shanley had been properly placed in his assignment by those before him. Little did Law know that an abuse allegation had been levied against Shanley a quarter century earlier, in 1966.[8]

Cardinal Law would later write of the Shanley case:

> "When I arrived in Boston in 1984, I assumed that priests in place had been appropriately appointed. It did not enter into my mind to second-guess my predecessors, and it simply was not in the culture of the day to function otherwise. Despite the quantity of documents released and statements on the part of some indicating they believe otherwise, before God I assure you that my first knowledge of an allegation of sexual abuse against this priest was in 1993. It was immediately acted upon, and the authorization for him to serve as a priest in California was rescinded. I was not aware until these recent months of allegations against him from as early as 1966.

> "In 1990, when Fr. Shanley left Boston [to live in Southern California], it was at his request that he was given a sick leave. It had nothing to do with an issue of sexual abuse. The attestation that he was a priest in good standing at the time was in accord with the facts as I knew them then."[9]

NOTES

[1] For example, one such contemporaneous account is from Daniel Tsang, "Men & Boys," *Gaysweek*, February 13, 1979.

[2] Handwritten archdiocesan notes following Shanley's treatment at The Institute of Living, March 3, 1994.

[3] Notable *Globe* articles about Shanley over the years include a lengthy Sunday *Globe* magazine feature, "The Homosexual, the Catholic Church, and Dignity," by Kay Longcope, July 22, 1973; Also:

"Priest cites wide discontent, criticizes Catholic hierarchy," by Stephen Kirkjian, April 25, 1969;

"2 priests attack Church rules on homosexuality," by Kay Longcope, March 10, 1974;

"Priest told to end ministry for homosexuals," by James Franklin, p. 3, February 2, 1979; and

"Catholic gays claim diocese ignores them," by Alan Sipress, on the *Globe*'s front page, August 29, 1982.

[4] Michael Paulson, "Heavy blow to Cardinal's credibility," *The Boston Globe*, April 8, 2002, p. A1.

[5] While there were no written complaints of sex abuse by Shanley in the 1980s, a woman named Jackie Gauvreau has claimed that she approached Cardinal Law following a Mass at her parish in 1984 to report an allegation of abuse by Shanley from 1981. It later turned out that Law never even visited the woman's parish in 1984. The earliest such an episode could have occurred was in 1987. Law has since responded: "[I]t has been reported that someone alleges I was informed after Mass in 1984 [*sic*] that Father Shanley had molested a child. I have absolutely no memory of such a conversation, and

those who have worked most closely with me can attest that such a report would have been acted upon. There is no record of that having happened, and furthermore, I had no suspicion about Fr. Shanley concerning this in the ensuing years." Cardinal Law to the people of the Archdiocese of Boston, Pentecost Sunday letter, May 19/20, 2002. … Also: Gauvreau apparently never called the police to report Shanley's 1981 abuse, but that did not stop her from boldly claiming in 2013, while running for office of mayor of Newton (an upscale Boston suburb), "I spent 25 years putting away a pedophile who had been active since 1967." Video of her statement is posted at Village14.com, dated August 27, 2013.

6 Paul Shanley's assignment record can be found at BishopAccountability.org.

7 Most Reverend Thomas V. Daily (Acting as Administrator of the Archdiocese) to Fr. Paul Shanley, letter dated November 4, 1983. (Cardinal Medeiros died on September 17, 1983.)

8 Shanley denied the accusation that he performed a manual sex act on a teenage boy.

9 Cardinal Law to the people of the Archdiocese of Boston, Pentecost Sunday letter, May 19/20, 2002.

25

Trial By Press Conference

There is more to that April 2002 press conference held by Roderick MacLeish about Fr. Paul Shanley, and the *Globe* misled its readers by leaving out a big part of the story in its coverage of the event.

As MacLeish stood on the stage at the Sheraton Hotel railing against the Church's handling of the Shanley case, he exhibited all of the outrage of a man who had only recently come to learn about the past crimes of Shanley.

In truth, however, eight years earlier, in 1994, MacLeish participated in a number of secret monetary settlements with the Archdiocese of Boston involving men who had claimed that Shanley had abused them decades earlier as teenagers.[1]

In other words, as MacLeish stood at the microphone and decried that Shanley had been "a monster in the Archdiocese of Boston for many, many years,"[2] he was ranting about a case he had already been aware of for many years.

A decade earlier, in 1992, the *Globe* showered major coverage upon MacLeish when he represented many victims in the much-publicized case of James Porter, an abusive priest from the neighboring Diocese of Fall River, who had left the priesthood back in 1972.

As a result of this high-profile case, MacLeish came to have close knowledge of the efforts of the Church in combatting abuse. And in subsequent years, MacLeish repeatedly *praised* the efforts of Cardinal Law and the Archdiocese of Boston for their work in addressing clergy abuse and reaching out to victims.

"I have to give them credit," MacLeish told the *Globe* in 1998. "They are doing a much better job."[3]

And after a public event in March of 2000 where Cardinal Law yet again profusely apologized for the sins of abusive priests and sought healing for victims, MacLeish cited the "extraordinary efforts" that Cardinal Law and the archdiocese had taken in trying to rectify the past and reach out to those harmed by abusive clergy:

> "It's another message of healing that's consistent with the extraordinary efforts the archdiocese has taken over the past eight years. A lot of people would say, 'Too little, too late.' I'm not one of them, because they're not just talking the talk, they're also walking the walk."[4]

But only two years later, MacLeish would be singing a much different tune and completing contradicting what he had publicly proclaimed only a short time earlier. When new accusers came forward in 2002, MacLeish executed a complete turnabout and began to regularly lambaste the Church.

Yet in all of its frenetic coverage of MacLeish's high-powered press conference, the *Globe* never once addressed MacLeish's abrupt flip-flop in thinking. Go figure.

"Secret settlements"?

The way the media has told it, Catholic dioceses somehow strong-armed victims into agreeing to monetary settlements that contained confidentiality clauses that demanded that the victims never speak publicly about their abuse. The *Globe* and mainstream media have often referred to such arrangements as "secret settlements."

The narrative asserts that years ago the Church somehow sought these arrangements as a way to "cover up" the crimes of its abusive priests by insisting that victims keep quiet about their abuse. The *Boston Globe* took this account one step further with the dark claim that the Archdiocese of Boston had somehow kept "tales of abuse out of the public eye through an elaborate culture of secrecy, decepetion [*sic*], and intimidation."[5]

However, as is often the case with the *Globe* and Catholic Church sex abuse story, the truth is an entirely different matter.

In fact, it was almost always the *victims* who demanded that the Church keep quiet about the abuse they had suffered and the settlements they made with the Church.

The Honorable Patrick J. Schiltz is now a federal judge for the United States District Court in Minnesota. Yet when he served in private practice in the 1980s and 1990s, he was involved in "over 500 clergy sexual misconduct cases in almost all fifty states and in several foreign countries," entailing "just about every Christian denomination in the United States."[6] Few men have had more experience with clergy cases than Schiltz.

And while Schiltz has been quite critical in the way bishops handled cases of abuse years ago, he blows the lid off the common story in the media about so-called "secret settlements." For starters:

"I have been involved in hundreds of settlements, and I literally cannot recall one that required the victim not to talk about his or her abuse."[7]

And in the uncommon instances that there were secrecy components, Schiltz has noted that it was usually the *victim* who requested secrecy:

"There is a reason why victims often sue as 'Jane Doe' or 'John Doe' and often seek protective orders from courts. Victims are understandably concerned to protect their privacy. That concern does not go away when the case is settled."[8]

Schiltz has also exposed some of the unseemly tactics of contingency lawyers who sue the Church:

"[I]t was plaintiffs' lawyers who would sometimes call church attorneys and say that, unless they were paid an outrageous amount, they would file a complaint against the church and call a press conference to publicize it. It was plaintiffs' lawyers who would sometimes make two settlement demands – a lower demand that did not include a secrecy agreement and a higher demand that did. It was plaintiffs' lawyers who would happily sell secrecy and happily take their 40-percent cut of the price of that secrecy. And yet some of these same plaintiffs' lawyers now tell reporters how very, very wrong it was for churches to buy what they were selling."[9]

Indeed, early on in its 2002 coverage, on February 1, *Globe* columnist Derrick Z. Jackson published a high-profile column wildly claiming that Cardinal Law and the Archdiocese of Boston had somehow "worked overtime" in strong-arming victims into agreeing to secret settlements.[10]

It would not be until one measly article on a Monday in June of 2002 – long after the media frenzy had raged for months – that the *Globe* finally exposed the truth of the matter: It was lawyers like Mitchell Garabedian and Roderick MacLeish, and *not* the Church, who had insisted on "secret settlements" and had implored complete silence from the Church.

The *Globe* reported that Garabedian "harbors no regrets about the settlements he negotiated in secrecy, often at his clients' insistence."

"They (his clients) were embarrassed," Garabedian told the *Globe*, "and many victims thought they were the only ones."[11]

But by June of 2002, the *Globe* and the rest of the media had already duped the public into believing that the confidential settlements had been insisted upon by the Church, not the other way around.

Paul J. Martinek, editor and publisher of *Lawyers Weekly* USA, told the *Globe*:

"Plaintiff lawyers settle cases confidentially all the time. But if you know your client's been raped by a priest and you settle the case confidentially, knowing that the priest could go out and do it again, your hands aren't entirely clean."[12]

NOTES

[1] Daniel Lyons, "Sex, God & Greed," *Forbes*, June 9, 2003.
[2] Walter V. Robinson and Thomas Farragher, "Shanley's record long ignored," *The Boston Globe*, April 9, 2002.
[3] Diego Ribadeneira and William F. Doherty, "Church pays priest's accusers," *The Boston Globe*, June 4, 1998, p. B1.
[4] Michael Paulson, "Law asks for atonement for sins of Catholics," *The Boston Globe*, March 12, 2000.
[5] See http://www.boston.com/globe/spotlight/abuse/scandal/. The misspelling is still on the site as of April 2015.
[6] Patrick J. Schiltz, "The Impact of Clergy Sexual Misconduct Litigation on Religious Liberty," *Boston College Law Review* (vol. 44, issue 4, article 2), July 1, 2003.
[7] Patrick J. Schiltz, "Not all the news is fit to print: What the media missed in the sexual-abuse scandal," *Commonweal*, August 15, 2003.
[8] Ibid.
[9] Ibid.
[10] Derrick Z. Jackson, "Law's lawyers worked overtime for secret settlements," *The Boston Globe*, February 1, 2002, p. A19.
[11] Sacha Pfeiffer, "Critical eye cast on sex abuse lawyers: Confidentiality, large settlements are questioned," *The Boston Globe*, June 3, 2002, p. A1.
[12] Ibid.

26

A Questionable Case

While the priesthood of Paul Shanley was indeed troubling, it does not mitigate the fact that the *Boston Globe* grossly misled its readers about the Shanley case. As a result of the cultural witch hunt that the *Globe* propagated, there is very strong evidence to conclude that Shanley was accused and tried for abuse he actually never committed.

On April 29, 2002, the *Globe* printed what may have been its most irresponsible article in all of its 2002 coverage. Penned by the Spotlight Team's Walter V. Robinson under the headline, "An alleged victim is called negligent," the article reported that in a reply to an abuse lawsuit against the Archdiocese, Cardinal Law had claimed that "a 6-year-old [was] responsible for his own sexual abuse."[1]

Once again, such a claim would be shocking if it were true. But it was most certainly not.

Robinson was writing about the case of Rodney and Paula Ford and their son, Greg. In their lawsuit against the Church, the Fords claimed that Fr. Shanley had somehow repeatedly abused Greg on practically a weekly basis for *seven years*, from age 6 to 13. According to the Fords' story, Shanley would repeatedly remove Greg and other boys in the middle of their Sunday school classes to take them away and molest them.

The result of the repeated abuse by Shanley, the Fords claimed, was that Greg had become a seriously troubled individual beset with profound mental illness and drug dependency.

As for the archdiocese's response to the Fords' lawsuit, the Church merely claimed that it was not the source of Greg's troubles. Law simply contended that any personal troubles were of his own doing, not from anything the Church did. The archdiocese's reply said nothing about a 6-year-old being responsible for his own abuse.

And as far as the Fords' claims of abuse by Shanley, Robinson left out several important parts the story.

For starters, Robinson never told readers of his article that Greg Ford originally *denied* to his parents that Shanley had ever abused him. In fact, one at a deposition there was even testimony that Greg had once claimed that his own father had raped him. In addition, a doctor treating Ford in an institution once wrote, "Patient revealed being sexually molested by neighbor and cousin(s) for about 3 years ages 7 to 9."[2] Nothing was recorded about abuse by a priest.

Most notably, the *Globe*'s Robinson did not report that the Fords' claims of abuse were entirely rooted in the bogus psychological theory of "repressed memory." The Fords incredibly claimed that after each time Shanley allegedly "fondled, sodomized, and otherwise sexually assaulted [Greg],"[3] Greg would actually *completely bury the memory* of the attack ever happening shortly after each episode. Greg would then repeatedly return to Sunday school week after week, and the assaults would continue unabated, the Fords' story goes.

If such a claim sounds implausible, if not outright

preposterous, it is because almost every reputable expert in the field of memory debunks such a scenario even being possible. (See more on "repressed memories" on pages 145-148.)

And if any theory asserting Shanley's innocence in the crimes of abusing young children sounds like some wild-eyed conspiracy to defend the Catholic Church, the fact is that questions about Shanley's case and challenges about its reporting have actually come from the media's most *liberal* sectors.

JoAnn Wypijewski is a veteran journalist who was once a senior editor at *The Nation*, an avowed liberal publication. She has also written for liberal publications such as *Mother Jones*, *Harper's*, *CounterPunch*, *The New York Times Magazine*, and *The Guardian* (UK), all of which are hardly friendly to the Catholic Church.

In a 2005 article for *CounterPunch* magazine, "The Passion of Paul Shanley," Wypijewski laid out a comprehensive and compelling case that Shanley is almost certainly innocent of the crimes for which he was accused of and convicted.

> "[Accuser Greg Ford] has had a hard time in life. He has been in 17 mental institutions or halfway houses. At age 11, he began drinking; he has also used anabolic steroids, cocaine, LSD, and other drugs. He has threatened his father with a knife and a metal pipe, assaulted a girlfriend, burned a local field, and threatened to kill his whole family and burn down the house …
>
> "[Ford and another accuser who invoked 'repressed memory'] say Father Shanley regularly pulled them out of CCD, sometimes as often as every week, between 1983 and 1989. All of the criminal activity would have occurred before the 10 o'clock Sunday Mass. Until Gregory Ford

came forward, none of the thousands of children who attended CCD at St. Jean's while Shanley was pastor reported anything untoward. No one is on record at the time as having noticed anything unusual involving the boys and Shanley. Not their parents. Not the several women who taught the classes, including Ford's mother. Not Verona Mazzei, the woman who supervised the program."

In other words, there was more than enough doubt to question the Fords' claims, yet not a shred of this doubt ever appeared in Robinson's April 2002 article in the *Globe.*

And remember that huge April 2002 press conference presented by lawyer Roderick MacLeish about Shanley? (See Chapter 25.) Wypijewski sees the roots of the Shanley hysteria in that very press conference:

> "So much of what is publicly known about Paul Shanley has its origin in a two-and-a-half-hour press conference that MacLeish held in April 2002 …
>
> "Following that press conference, it was reported that Shanley's file reveals a 30-year pattern of accusations of sexual abuse, cover-ups, and transfers of the priest from parish to parish. That they contain an admission by Shanley of rape as well as the results of a psychiatric examination showing that 'his pathology is beyond repair.' That they indicate Shanley was a founding member of the North American Man/Boy Love Association. That they show he left St. Jean's in 1989 because of sex abuse charges, and was transferred to California although the church knew he was a child molester. Those claims, repeatedly recycled, created a portrait of the priest as criminal before any legal charge was made. **Not one of them is supported by**

documents in the file."[4]

Indeed, Wypijewski is entirely correct. So much of what was reported about the Shanley case was simply false. (For example, Shanley was not a "founding member of NAMBLA." And the psychiatrist who said that Shanley's "pathology (was) beyond repair" had never even met Shanley; he was referring not to any abuse by Shanley but to his alleged "laziness."[5])

In the end, the Fords' charges against Shanley were so wild and flimsy that law enforcement actually dropped the Fords as witnesses in its criminal case against the priest.

After studying the Shanley case, one legal observer would later claim, "The record in *Commonwealth v. Shanley* documents the most egregious case of gross negligence, incompetence, and greed that I have seen in practicing law in several dozen jurisdictions over many years."[6]

"Repressed memories"?

One seriously underreported element of the narrative that is the Catholic Church abuse scandals is that many alleged victims have surfaced with their charges after claiming they "repressed" memories of their abuse for periods of years, often decades, and then "recovered" them.

As always, we must be mindful and sensitive in dealing with this subject. Of course, not all victims of clergy abuse claim "recovered memory." The pain of sexual abuse is all too devastatingly real.

What almost all journalists have failed to report, however, is that there is no scientific evidence that "recovered memory" is genuine at all. In fact, many experts in the field of psychology and memory science have flat-out discredited the theory.

"Recovered-memory therapy will come to be recognized as the quackery of the 20th century," Richard Ofshe, a social psychologist at the University of California, Berkeley, has said.[7]

"If penis envy made us look dumb, this will make us look totally gullible," adds Paul McHugh, chairman of the psychiatry department at Johns Hopkins University.[8]

The truth is that people who have remembered their childhood abuse their whole lives have a clearer and more detailed memory of being abused. They also report more intense feelings.[9] This science is in line with studies involving Holocaust survivors and war veterans. These studies have consistently found that "the difficulty for those people is not remembering their ordeals, but forgetting them."[10]

After a six-year study, Harvard psychology professor Richard J. McNally wrote a book about memory and child abuse called *Remembering Trauma*.[11] "The notion that the mind protects itself by banishing the most disturbing, terrifying events is psychiatric folklore," McNally has said. "The more traumatic and stressful something is, the less likely someone is to forget it."[12]

"The notion that traumatic events can be repressed and later recovered is the most pernicious bit of folklore ever to infect psychology and psychiatry. It has provided the theoretical basis for 'recovered memory therapy' – the worst catastrophe to befall the mental health field since the lobotomy era."[13]

Dr. James McGaugh is from the University of California, Irvine. His expertise in the area of memory was once profiled on CBS' *60 Minutes* program. Regarding the issue of "repressed memory," Dr. McGaugh said in a 2010 book,

"I do not believe there's such a thing as repressed memory. I haven't seen a single instance in which a memory was completely repressed and popped up again.

"I go on science, not fads. And there's absolutely no proof that it can happen. Zero. None. Niente. Nada. All my research says that strong emotional experiences leave emotionally strong memories. Being sexually molested would certainly qualify."[14]

Yet because of the alliances between journalists, victim lawyers, and advocacy groups, the debunked theory of "repressed memory" remains almost universally unchallenged in our nation's media.

Elizabeth Loftus, professor of psychology at the University of California Irvine, has been dubbed "the most influential female psychologist of the past century," and she may be the world's leading researcher on memory.[15] Her years of work debunking the theory of repressed memory has made her not only an authority, but her work has enabled individuals falsely accused of awful sex crimes to be exonerated.

Dr. Loftus has numerous studies to her credit that show that memories can be distorted. She has also demonstrated that totally false memories can be planted in people's minds. For example, in experiments Dr. Loftus has been able to plant the false memories of "getting lost for an extended time as a child, facing a threat to one's life as a child, witnessing demonic possession as a child, seeing wounded animals as part of a traumatic bombing, and more."[16] Loftus' book, authored with Katherine Ketchum, *The Myth of Repressed Memory*,[17] is very well known and respected in the psychology field.

"Memory can be changed, inextricably altered, and that what we think we know, what we believe with all our hearts, is not necessarily the truth," says Dr. Loftus.[18] As for the claim that people are able to "repress" traumatic events, she says, "You can't be raped for 10 years and not remember it. Yet, according to the repression aficionados, anything's possible."[19]

In a 2003 column in the *Boston Globe*, columnist Eileen McNamara addressed the Paul Shanley case in which recovered-memory therapy played an important role. McNamara snipped, "It defies belief, but not possibility, that the Catholic Church in Boston intends to suggest in court that this scandal is nothing but a figment of the victims' imagination."[20]

The Church never claimed, of course, that the *entire scandal* was "nothing but a figment of the victims' imagination," but in this particular case, lawyers for Shanley asserted that the accuser's claim was untrue.

When there is no science to support recovered-memory therapy, McNamara exemplifies the sort of crooked rhetoric that some journalists have resorted to.

NOTES

1 Walter V. Robinson, "An alleged victim is called negligent," *The Boston Globe*, April 29, 2002, p. A1.
2 JoAnn Wypijewski, "The Passion of Paul Shanley," *CounterPunch*, January 29-31, 2005.
3 Ibid.
4 Ibid.
5 Michael Miner, "Did Shanley Get Screwed?" *Chicago Reader*, February 17, 2005.
6 P. Johannes Ehrat, SJ, *Power of Scandal: Semiotic and Pragmatic in Mass Media* (Toronto: University of Toronto Press, Scholarly Publishing Division, 2011), p. 367.
7 Leon Jaroff and Jeanne McDowell, "Repressed-Memory Therapy: Lies of the Mind," *Time*, November 29, 1993.
8 Ibid.
9 Loftus, E.F., Polonsky, S., & Fullilove, M. T. (1994). Memories of childhood sexual abuse: Remembering and repressing. *Psychology of Women Quarterly*, 18, 67-845.
10 Benjamin Radford, "Validity of 'Repressed Memories' Challenged in Court," *LiveScience*, September 15, 2009.
11 Richard J. McNally, *Remembering Trauma* (Cambridge, Mass.: Belknap Press of Harvard University Press), 2005.
12 Daniel Lyons, "Sex, God & Greed," *Forbes*, June 9, 2003.
13 "Richard McNally Amicus Letter," June 3, 2005. Addressed to Honorable Ronald M. George, Chief Justice and Associate Justices of the California Supreme Court. Re: *Nicole Taus vs. Elizabeth Loftus et al.* (1st D.C.A. Civ No. A104689, Solano County Superior Court No. FCS02A557).
14 Meredith Moran, *My Lie: A True Story of False Memory* (San Francisco: Jossey-Bass), 2010, p. 223.
15 Amy Wilson, "War & remembrance," *Orange County Register*, November 3, 2002.
16 "Elizabeth F. Loftus: Award for Distinguished Scientific Applications of Psychology," *American Psychologist*, Vol. 58, No. 11, 2003, p. 865.
17 Elizabeth Loftus and Katherine Ketchum, *The Myth of Repressed Memories* (New York: St. Martin's Griffin), 1994.

---

[18] Elizabeth Loftus, "Dear Mother: Facing the Loss of a Parent: The personal story of losing a parent," *Psychology Today*, May 1, 2003.

[19] Sasha Abramsky, "Memory and Manipulation: The trials of Elizabeth Loftus, defender of the wrongly accused," *LA Weekly*, August 19, 2004.

[20] Eileen McNamara, "Still Catholic, but changed," *Boston Globe*, March 9, 2003.

27

From Reality to Caricature

By the time Cardinal Law resigned in December of 2002, the *Globe* had doggedly crafted a depiction of the Archbishop of Boston which was warped from reality. Indeed, a casualty of the *Globe*'s relentless coverage was the truth about who Cardinal Law really was as a man and as a bishop. While Cardinal Law's handling of the scandals was certainly deserving of just scrutiny, the *Globe*'s reporting was something else entirely.

No individual, even Cardinal Law himself, would argue that he handled abuse cases perfectly. But the *Globe*'s ultimate depiction of Law as a cleric who was callous to the plight of victims and insensitive to the realities of sex abuse by priests was not only grossly unfair, but ultimately false.

When Bernard Law first arrived in Massachusetts in March of 1984 to serve as Archbishop of Boston, he brought with him an awe-inspiring record of public service and personal accomplishment. Born in Mexico in 1931 into a family with a father who worked for the United States Army and the aviation industry, Law experienced an uncommon childhood which involved moving frequently. By the time he finished high school, Law had "lived in Mexico, Colombia,

Panama, and the Virgin Islands, with occasional periods of residence in the mainland United States."[1]

After graduating from Harvard University, Law entered the seminary in 1953. By the time he was 29, he was ordained as a priest in the Diocese of Natchez-Jackson, Mississippi.

Law's first assignment was at a parish in the coastal town of Vicksburg, Mississippi, where one local man would later observe that Father Law "went into homes as priests had never done before," ministering to the ill and afflicted.[2]

But it was the cause of civil rights for black people into which Law threw himself. In the early 1960s in Mississippi, being a white person championing civil rights often meant putting one's life in danger. And being a Catholic did not help matters either, as Catholics were often targets of the Ku Klux Klan.

As black civil rights leaders were being gunned down in 1963 and 1964, Law used the diocesan newspaper to scold local government leaders for their failure to stand up to racists.[3] In return, racists issued death threats to Father Law[4], and many advertisers cancelled their business with the diocesan newspaper, slashing its revenue.[5]

Law remained determined, however. The young priest established an interfaith organization, the Mississippi Council on Human Relations, as a multi-pronged force to tackle racism. In a short time, Baptists, Catholics, Episcopalians, Jews, white people, and black people all joined together in the fight for justice and dignity.

So influential was Father Law that some black residents converted to Catholicism and specifically cited Law for doing so. And another resident who worked with Law in the civil rights struggle concluded, "I think he has had more influence on the Church in Mississippi than anyone in the last 100 years."[6]

Charles Evers, the brother of the slain civil rights leader Medgar Evers, would soon exclaim:

> "We feel that Father Law is not just a priest; he's a great humanitarian. If it had not been for Father Law, our problems wouldn't be as far along in being solved as they are. He has done it not for the Negro, but for justice and what is right."[7]

In the 1970s, while stationed in Missouri, Bishop Law continued his advocacy, but in a different manner. After becoming aware of a Vietnamese refugee camp of religious men in Arkansas, he personally arranged and invited the men to take shelter in a seminary.[8]

When Law arrived in Boston years later, he quickly built a reputation as a crusader in the fights for "racial harmony, interfaith cooperation and social justice."[9] He also continued his fight against bigotry, urging public integration of public housing in Boston when many stood against it.[10]

And even though gay activists would protest and pelt the Cardinal with condoms and epithets over his so-called "callousness" to AIDS victims, he not only fought to secure affordable shelter for those stricken with AIDS,[11] but he also met privately with those suffering from AIDS to minister to them.[12] (File under: "No good deed goes unpunished.")

Cardinal Law was also a vocal force on behalf of the poor, as he often challenged his fellow clerics in their responsibility to work in feeding and clothing the hungry and needy.[13] And while some wild-eyed critics of the Church would often try to portray Law as a "conservative" because of his social views, the truth is that Cardinal Law often argued in favor of a strong government role in serving the poor. A

December 2000 article began:

> "As the [Massachusetts Governor Paul] Cellucci administration trumpets the successes of welfare reform, Cardinal Bernard F. Law is painting a different picture, saying that poor families are struggling and the state should do more to help them.
>
> "'We oppose government's diminished role in helping families overcome poverty and meet their children's basic needs,' Law, the Roman Catholic archbishop of Boston, wrote in a letter … 'The target of welfare reform ought to be poverty, not poor families'."[14]

Law also worked to improve relations in the Boston area between the Catholic Church and local Jewish people. After arriving in Boston, Law soon allied himself Jewish leader Leonard Zakim, the Boston Regional Director of the Anti-Defamation League, and over the years the two would often join forces in the crusade against bias. When gay activists assaulted priests at the 1990 ordination ceremony in Boston (see Chapter 7), Zakim joined Catholics in their outrage against the attacks.[15]

As the Archbishop of Boston, Cardinal Law also achieved amazing diplomatic successes overseas. It is widely believed that Law played a crucial role in making Pope John Paul II's historic 1998 trip to Cuba possible.

Starting in the 1980s, Law made several diplomatic trips to the island nation, often meeting with Fidel Castro with the hope that he would allow the Church to operate openly in the officially atheist country. On one trip in 1997, Law brought 3,800 pounds of medicine with him.[16] Meanwhile, Law openly criticized the United States' policy of sanctions against Cuba.[17]

In large part due to Law's efforts, the Church began to minister more freely in Cuba, and after Pope Benedict XVI returned to the country in March of 2012, Cuba declared Good Friday, which was occurring a week later, to be a public holiday. (In 2014, Cuba – a country which officially declared itself to be atheist in 1959 – decided that Good Friday should be a national holiday *every* year.)

Just plain wrong

Another notable low over the years in the *Boston Globe*'s nasty coverage of the Catholic Church occurred in a December 14, 1989, column by David Nyhan, entitled, "Cardinals' silence on Jesuits' slayings."[18]

In his article, Nyhan suggested that President George H.W. Bush had influenced Cardinal Law and four other American cardinals to remain silent over his administration's handling of the murders of six Jesuit priests in El Salvador in exchange for a speech supporting the Church's pro-life efforts.

Quite simply, Nyhan's claim was flat-out false.

In truth, Cardinal Law had already condemned the killings in El Salvador weeks earlier in a November 24, 1989, column he wrote for *The Pilot*, the weekly newspaper of the Archdiocese of Boston.[19]

And as for the other four cardinals whom Nyhan accused of remaining silent, they, too, had already issued statements condemning the killings.[20]

The next day following the *Globe*'s bogus attack, Cardinal Law slammed Nyhan's article as "slanderous." Law then added, quite notably:

"Unfortunately, this is not the first time that the pages of the *Globe* have misrepresented facts concerning or of interest to the Catholic Church. Efforts have been made at all levels and in various ways to address this matter, but to no avail."[21]

Indeed, many years before its 2002 coverage, the *Globe*'s exhibited that accurate and honest journalism did not apply when reporting about the Catholic Church.

NOTES

1 Romanus Cessario, C.P., (2002). *Boston's Cardinal.* Lanham, Maryland: Lexington Books. This book is a collection of some of Cardinal Law's notable writings – over 80 of them. The citation is from page xvi of the book, from a biographical introduction by Mary Ann Glendon.

2 Ibid., p. xxii (Glendon).

3 Ibid., p. xxiii (Glendon).

4 Charles N. Bransom, "Harvard's first Cardinal – Bernard Law," *The Pilot*, November 4, 2011, p. 21.

5 W.F. Minor, "Father Law: A Force in Mississippi Integration,"

The Virgin Islands Daily News, April 22, 1966, p. 13.
6 Minor, p. 15.
7 Ibid.
8 Bransom.
9 Steve Marantz, "Many praise Law's work for justice, harmony," *The Boston Globe*, April 25, 1985, p. 15.
10 Doris Sue Wong, "Cardinal Law urges peaceful integration of South Boston housing," *The Boston Globe*, January 25, 1988.
11 David Nyhan, "How a good priest became a bad guy in court and in the press," *The Boston Globe*, January 2, 1999, p. A14.
12 Michael Paulson, "Scandal eclipses a far-reaching record," *The Boston Globe*, December 14, 2002, p. A1.
13 James L. Franklin, "Law asks all to help the needy," *The Boston Globe*, June 5, 1985, p. 86.
14 Michael Paulson, "Cardinal points to city's poor: Statistics don't tell full story of families off welfare, he says," *The Boston Globe*, December 6, 2000, p. A15.
15 Leonard Zakim, "Appalling lack of respect for sanctity of ordination," *The Pilot*, June 22, 1990, p. 12. Also of note: Mere weeks before he died from bone-marrow cancer in 1999, Zakim travelled to Rome, where Pope John Paul II named Zakim a knight to the Papal Order of St. Gregory to recognize his career commitment to fighting bigotry. Although this knighthood is not usually granted to non-Catholics, the *Globe* gave this remarkable event only passing mention.
16 Diego Ribadeneira, "Cardinal Law raps US policy on Cuba, *The Boston Globe*, April 11, 1997, p. A2.
17 Diego Ribadeneira, "Cardinal Law raps US policy on Cuba, *The Boston Globe*, April 11, 1997, p. A2.
18 David Nyhan, "Cardinals' silence on Jesuits' slayings," *The Boston Globe*, December 1, 1989.
19 Cardinal Bernard Law, "Nothing can justify such inhumane acts," *The Pilot*, November 24, 1989, p. 2.
20 James L. Franklin, "Cardinal Law silent on aid to El Salvador," *The Boston Globe*, December 19, 1989. [It should also be noted that in 1992 Cardinal Law again opposed President George H.W. Bush, this time for his administration's decision to turn back refugees from Haiti. "In the name of all that is decent, we cannot turn our back on poor Haitians willing to take heroic measures in order to

escape a hopeless situation," said Cardinal Law. Source: Franklin, James L., "The cardinal and the news media," *The Boston Globe*, May 29, 1992, p. 24.]

[21] Alexander Reid, "Cardinal attacks Globe for column," *The Boston Globe*, December 15, 1989, p. 45.

28

Unstoppable

Is there anything that Cardinal Law could have done in 2002 to show amends for his past handling of abuse cases and placate those at the *Boston Globe*? Is there anything that Cardinal Law could have done that would have quelled the paper's relentlessness in pursuing its story?

In a nutshell: No.

For many years leading up to the paper's 2002 coverage of the sex abuse story, writers at the *Globe* demonstrated that Cardinal Law and the Catholic Church were in their crosshairs, and there was nothing that Law and the Church could do to stop them, facts be damned.

For example, *Globe* columnist Eileen McNamara began a November 1992 review about a book on Catholic sex abuse as follows:

> "When reports surfaced last spring that a former Massachusetts priest had allegedly molested scores of schoolchildren at a Fall River parish, Cardinal Bernard F. Law was silent about the Church's culpability but fierce in his denunciation of the media for focusing 'on the faults of a few'."[1]

The average reader never would have known it, but McNamara's opener was simply false. In fact, a number of times in 1992, Cardinal Law acknowledged the scourge of abuse that wrecked the innocence of victims and wreaked immense harm upon the Church. He also recognized the clear role the Church played in the abuse of children.

Months before McNamara's column, in one of a number of columns he penned in 1992 to address the issue of clergy abuse, Law wrote, "It is difficult to imagine a more tragic situation than to have a person, particularly a child, betrayed and abused by a priest."

"Any act of abuse, because of the harm done the victim, is abhorrent," Cardinal Law added. "My desire, often expressed to my closest collaborators, is to *deal* with problems, not hide them."[2]

In another missive that year, the Cardinal wrote about the immense betrayal that victims often speak of when talking about their abuse. Law articulated the "disastrous effect of all such acts on the families of victims" and reiterated that abuse by members of Catholic clergy was a "heinous crime." He also added:

> "Such behavior (abuse) always involves the betrayal of the trust of the Church … The Church is plunged into an understandable self-examination to ensure that as best as is humanly possible such acts are dealt with responsibly …
>
> "My frustration and anger is in the fact of an awful sense of betrayal of trust which has done terrible injury to children, to their families, and all of us."[3]

In other words, McNamara's attack was simply bogus.

And it was also in 1992 that Cardinal Law ordered the formation of a special review board to examine accusations against priests. In January 1993, Law officially installed the board, which included women, lay people, and experts in child sex abuse. He also strengthened, published, and publicized the archdiocese's policy for handling sex abuse cases. Law would also add:

> "Sexual misconduct with a minor is a tragedy which understandably gives rise to repugnance and outrage. The Archdiocese is committed to do all it can to ensure that children being served by the Church are not placed at risk. We also want to take those steps which can facilitate healing."[4]

Upon the announcement of the new review board and its revamped policies, even Roderick MacLeish, the most high-profile Church-suing lawyer in Boston at the time, admitted that he was pleased with the Cardinal Law's efforts. He was happy to see lay people serving on the review board, and he acknowledged of the archdiocese's measures, "On the whole, not bad."[5]

By the end of 1993, Cardinal Law's review board had removed **20** accused priests from active ministry and put them on indefinite leave. And yet again, lawyer MacLeish *praised* these measures and, according to the *Globe*, "credited the Catholic Archdiocese of Boston with taking prompt action on the accusations."[6]

At the time, **no one** complained that Law did not disclose the actual names of the 20 priests. Neither did anyone bemoan an alleged "lack of transparency" from the Church, as many would decry years later.

Instead, Cardinal Law's measures were soon seen as a

model for how to handle accusations. Despite the animosity toward the Church in the media, one would be hard-pressed to find anyone criticizing Cardinal Law in 1993 for the actions he took at the time.

And Cardinal Law continued his efforts in ensuing years to fight child abuse and reach out to victims. In the mid-1990s, when victims of abusive priest John Geoghan began to come forward publicly – reminding the Church once again of the incredible pain that his abuse had caused – Cardinal Law announced a series of healing Masses "to implore the healing of Jesus for the pain and suffering caused by the sexual abuse of children by clergy." The idea for the Masses came directly "out of conversations with victims."[7] Cardinal Law would say at the time (1997):

> "I know of nothing that has caused greater pain to the Church than this phenomenon of abuse. With all my heart I beg forgiveness of all who have been hurt by such acts as abuse."[8]

In June of 1998, when Cardinal Law announced the complete removal of Geoghan from the priesthood, he again lamented:

> "As long as I am archbishop I will be haunted by those persons who have been victimized."[9]

And in 1999, when law enforcement finally charged Geoghan for his crimes, Law again reiterated the truth of the immense suffering that abuse in the Church had caused:

> "Just one incident is enough to sadden and depress and sicken me …
>
> "In my 26 years as bishop, nothing has given me more

> anguish than have these cases. But whatever anguish I feel is unimportant … It's the anguish of people who have been betrayed by public persons …
> "[O]ne gets a sick feeling in the pit of one's stomach …
> "It's the violation of trust which is the worst thing. As I've dealt with victims I have felt that the most lingering pain is the violation of trust. That violation of trust very understandably gets transferred in terms of resentment and fear and anger to whatever the person, in this case the priest, represents."[10]

And in 2001, when news of Geoghan's abuse surfaced yet again, Law asserted:

> "The sexual abuse of minors by priests is one of the most painful problems facing the contemporary Church …
> "I can only imagine the anguish of heart experienced by the victims themselves and by their families. I know that nothing else has given me the anguish that I experience because of these cases."[11]

In other words, for many years before 2002, Cardinal Law made numerous genuine efforts to confront the issue of clergy sex abuse. And overall, abuse victims and the media considered these efforts to be all very positive.

Yet when the *Globe* unleashed its blitzkrieg against the Church in Boston in 2002, it was if Cardinal Law had made no efforts at all over the years.

With days after the *Globe*'s first story in January, media outlets across the nation were frenetic. Cardinal Law held a press conference to address the growing crisis and answer any questions asked of him. Even local television outlets preempted programming to carry Law's event live.

Adding to the media frenzy was an element that had

never even existed years earlier, and it enabled the *Globe* to spread their stories to every corner of the world: the Internet. Whereas before *Globe* stories would rarely extend beyond the geographical area of New England, the World Wide Web enabled countless other media outlets to relay the paper's stories far and wide. And thousands of eager forums were happy to oblige.

The Catholic sex abuse story was simply unstoppable.

Debunking an urban legend:
No, Cardinal Law did not "flee to the Vatican"

The way detractors tell it, one late night in early December of 2002, Massachusetts State troopers were pounding on the door of Cardinal Law's residence in Brighton, a neighborhood of Boston. They were armed with a subpoena for him to give a deposition and to account for crimes he had committed. But, lo and behold, they claim, His Eminence had already "fled to the Vatican," where he was forever "sheltered from prosecution."

Cardinal Law "escaped justice," these storytellers claim.

The problem? The story is bogus.

Indeed, state troopers were at the door on the night that Cardinal Law travelled to the Vatican to submit his resignation.

However, for obvious reasons, law enforcement does not notify citizens in advance when they will come knocking at their doors. So Cardinal Law would have had no idea that state troopers would have been serving a subpoena on any given night or on the night he went overseas.

In truth, as planned all along, Cardinal Law returned to Boston from Rome after submitting his resignation. In ensuing months, he complied with his subpoenas, sitting for numerous depositions in early 2003 giving grand jury testimony. (Many are also are unaware that the Cardinal Law spent a number of months in early 2003 in private retreat at St. Vincent Archabbey, a Benedictine monastery outside Pittsburgh.[12])

Quite simply, Cardinal Law complied with every court order he was asked to. And when Massachusetts Attorney General Thomas Reilly later completed his lengthy investigation into the Catholic Church in July 2003, he concluded, "The evidence gathered during the course of the Attorney General's sixteen-month investigation does not provide a basis for bringing criminal charges against the Archdiocese and its senior managers."[13]

But the facts have never stopped Church critics to propagate the myth that "Cardinal Law fled to the Vatican to escape prosecution." Mainstream media outlets and even famed commenters such as Christopher Hitchens and Peggy Noonan have helped spread the urban legend.[14]

More low blows from the *Globe*

Even years after playing a leading role in the resignation of Cardinal Law, the *Boston Globe* has continued to besmirch Law with its warped reporting.

A November 5, 2011, article in the *Globe* accused *The Pilot*, the official newspaper of the Archdiocese of Boston, of publishing a "lengthy article" that "honored" Cardinal Law on his 80th birthday.

The *Globe* predictably turned to "victims of clergy abuse, their lawyers, and advocates" who "condemned" the *Pilot* for printing such an article.

In truth, the article was not about celebrating Cardinal Law's birthday at all. The column was simply part of a series of weekly profiles celebrating the centennial of Boston's Archbishop William Henry O'Connell becoming a Cardinal. The profile of Law was merely part of this series about others who had served in Boston and had also become a cardinal in their lives.

And while the *Globe* characterized the profile of Law as a "lengthy story," the entire article only covered a *single page*.

Two paragraphs of the profile were dedicated to the tragedy of the abuse scandals, but the *Globe* trumpeted critics who claimed that the space was not enough, as if Law's lengthy and eventful career was supposed to be reduced to the scandals alone.

And in an entirely different episode altogether, while Cardinal Law was in Rome on his 80th birthday, he wanted to have a get-together at a local restaurant. The party was intended as a *private* affair for a small clique of fellow clerics and friends, but, predictably and unfortunately, the *Globe* and the rest of the mainstream media got wind of it.

The *Globe* and the media fell over themselves to try and portray the simple occasion as being much larger and lavish than it actually was. Judging from the *Globe*'s coverage alone, one would have thought that Law threw himself a swanky affair fit for King Henry VIII. The *Globe* decried the fact that the attendees actually enjoyed lasagna, prosciutto, and wine at the party. Imagine that. Lasagna. Prosciutto. Wine. At a birthday party. In Rome.

In the eyes of the *Globe*, even throwing oneself a private birthday party was an outrage. Of course.

NOTES

1 Eileen McNamara, "Inside the story that shook the church," *The Boston Globe*, November 3, 1992, p.29.
2 Bernard Cardinal Law, "How We Deal With Sexual Abuse," *The Pilot*, May 29, 1992, p.2.
3 Bernard Cardinal Law, "The Priesthood in Perspective," *The Pilot*, September 25, 1992, p. 2
4 "Cardinal Law Joins Church Leaders In Confronting Clerical Sexual Misconduct," *The Pilot*, January 22, 1993, p. 16.
5 David Arnold, "Archdiocese sets misconduct rules Review board to examine sexual abuse of minors," *The Boston Globe*, January 15, 1993, p. 22.
6 James L. Franklin, "Lawyer for Porter victims says 20 other priests in area are accused," *The Boston Globe*, December 9, 1993, p. 42.
7 Diego Ribadeneira, "Healing Masses set for victims of abuse by priests," *The Boston Globe*, October 10, 1997.

---

[8] Bernard Cardinal Law, "Lord, I am not worthy …" *The Pilot*, November 14, 1997, p. 2.
[9] Diego Ribadeneira, "Cardinal announces defrocking of priest," *The Boston Globe*, June 7, 1998, p. A1.
[10] Andrea Estes (quoting Cardinal Law), "Breach of trust: Law 'sickened' by child rape charges vs. Geoghan," *The Boston Herald*, December 3, 1999, pp. 1, 26.
[11] Bernard Cardinal Law, "Restoring hope to broken hearts and lives," *The Pilot*, July 27, 2001, p. 2.
[12] Associated Press, "Cardinal Law goes on private retreat," *The Boston Globe*, February 20, 2003.
[13] Thomas Reilly, "The Sexual Abuse of Children in the Roman Catholic Archdiocese of Boston: Executive Summary and Scope of Investigation," July 23, 2003.
[14] For Hitchens, see "Should The Pope Be Indicted? Can He?" by Ben Wofford, *Brown Political Review*, February 12, 2013; "Tear Down That Wall" by Christopher Hitchens, slate.com, March 22, 2010; and "The Pope Should Be Questioned in Sex-Abuse Cases" by Christopher Hitchens, *Newsweek*, April 22, 2010.
For Peggy Noonan, see "How to Save the Catholic Church," *Wall Street Journal*, April 17, 2010.

29

"The war is over"?

"The war is over."

With those four words in a column by Eileen McNamara in April of 2003, the *Boston Globe* openly admitted what many observers had largely suspected all along: that the *Globe* explicitly viewed its reporting about abuse by priests as part of a "war" against the Catholic Church.

McNamara's words were part of a story she penned about the Archdiocese of Boston refusing to accept a disingenuous donation from a dissident lay group that had formed as a result of the *Globe*'s reporting only 16 months earlier. McNamara declared, "The war is over," and then advised the group "to follow Vermont Senator George D. Aiken's advice to President Lyndon Johnson on Vietnam: Declare victory and leave."[1]

Indeed, by April of 2003, the *Globe* had certainly felt it could "declare victory." It was the month that the paper scored the much-coveted Pulitzer Prize, and the paper had inflicted serious damage upon the Catholic Church. Not only was the paper wildly successful in its efforts to oust Cardinal Law from his job, it had successfully managed to paint a caricature of the Catholic Church as an institution that was aloof to the plight of child molesters, out-of-touch with modern sensibilities, and rife with out-of-control pedophiles.

In doing so, the *Globe* truly accomplished what its ultimate goal was all along: to cripple the authority of the Church in speaking out on issues of public concern, especially on those in which the *Globe* stood in opposition.

Many people cannot help but think that it is no coincidence that only two years after the *Globe* initiated its all-out blitzkrieg against the Church, Massachusetts became the first state in the Union to legalize gay marriage in 2004. The Church in the Archdiocese of Boston was so weakened and reeling from the scandals that its voice against the crusade for gays was effectively muted. By 2003, without the strong platform of the Church in the discussion, the debate in the media was so one-sided that gay marriage in Massachusetts was all-but-inevitable.

Archbishop Seán P. O'Malley had replaced Cardinal Law in Boston in July of 2003, and although O'Malley possessed a unique touch with regards to pastoral matters, it was obvious that speaking out about "hot-button" issues in the Church was not his particular strength. The folks at the *Globe* must have been laughing on the floor on the day it received and agreed to publish an op-ed from O'Malley in March of 2004 that feebly asked Boston Catholics to merely "defend the institution of marriage with courage and charity."[2]

Indeed, while O'Malley made efforts to thwart the tide for gay marriage in Massachusetts, he was clearly both uncomfortable and ineffective in the role of doing so.

With the introduction of gay marriage in Massachusetts, the very same group that had cursed and tossed condoms at an ordination ceremony fourteen years earlier could now declare victory.

While McNamara was entirely correct that the *Globe* had been waging a war against the Catholic Church, she was wrong to say that the war is over.

Certainly the *Globe* won a major battle, but years later, it is now clear that the paper did not win the war.

A dozen years after the *Globe*'s landmark 2002 coverage, the Catholic Church is on the rebound. Following the firm leadership of Pope Benedict XVI, Pope Francis is reigniting the Catholic Church in an exciting manner. Pope Francis' call for Catholics to live out the Gospel of Jesus Christ is intriguing many who once thought they had abandoned their faith for good.

Many believe that for the first time in a century, the Catholic Church in Boston (and in the United States) only shows signs of getting stronger.

Meanwhile, the same cannot be said for the *Boston Globe*. Back in 1993, the New York Times Company purchased the *Globe* for an astonishing $1.1 billion, "among the highest prices paid for an American newspaper."[3] Only twenty years later, in 2013, a principal owner of the Boston Red Sox baseball team bought the paper for a paltry $70 million, only *6 percent* of what it was originally bought for by the Times in 1993. And one expert concluded that it was *Globe*'s *real estate* – not the actual paper itself – which was the true value in the purchase.

"From a strictly business standpoint, the real value here isn't selling newspapers or even the boston.com website," real estate expert Joseph Palermino told the *Boston Herald*. "I'd say the real value is more in the real estate."[4]

"[I]f the Globe were to fail as an ongoing business venture, the real estate is a great cushion to fall back on," another observer concluded.[5]

Indeed, as a business venture, the *Globe* continues to flounder. In November 2014, the *Globe* informed staffers that it was moving forward with the potential sale of its valuable headquarters in Boston's Dorchester neighborhood.[6]

Revenue at the paper has plummeted over the years. The *Globe* has slashed its workforce so many times[7] that the number of staffers at the paper is only a small fraction of what it once was many years earlier. The paper now aggressively seeks low-cost college interns to fill valuable roles in helping the newspaper function, including as general assignment reporters.[8]

That's right. *College interns* are now actual reporters for the *Boston Globe.*

How fitting.

NOTES

[1] Eileen McNamara, "This church won't budge," *The Boston Globe*, April 2, 2003, p. B1.
[2] Seán P. O'Malley, "Charity needed in debate on gay marriage," *The Boston Globe*, March 11, 2004, p. A19.
[3] Christine Haughney, "New York Times Company Sells Boston Globe," *The New York Times*, August 4, 2013, p. A15.
[4] Chris Cassidy, "Expert: Boston Globe building is best deal," *The Boston Herald*, July 2, 2013.
[5] Rick Edmonds, "7 things to know about The Boston Globe's sale to John Henry," poynter.com, August 4, 2013.
[6] Adam Vaccaro, "Boston Globe Negotiating to Sell Dorchester Property," boston.com, November 4, 2014.
[7] For example: "Boston Globe Dismantling National Staff," Maynard Institute (http://mije.org/), October 17, 2005; "Boston Globe cuts 24 from news staff, including Pulitzer Prize winners," Associated Press, March 22, 2007; Andrew Beaujon, "Boston Globe offers buyouts to employees, lays off 10," poynter.com, July

24, 2012; "Boston Globe Cuts Jobs in Newsroom, Elsewhere," nytexaminer.com, July 26, 2012; Jon Chesto, "The Boston Globe lays off six journalists who write for its Your Town sites," *Boston Business Journal*, September 12, 2013;

[8] Viewed at https://services.bostonglobe.com/aboutus/career/career.aspx?id=7282, (accessed January 3, 2015).

Index

Also by Dave Pierre:

Double Standard: Abuse Scandals and the Attack on the Catholic Church

"*Double Standard: Abuse Scandals and the Attack on the Catholic Church* is **essential reading** for anyone who wants to hear the other side of the clergy sexual abuse scandal ... Even for someone who has read about this subject for years, it was **eye-opening** to me ... If someone attacks you or slanders the Church over the sexual abuse scandal, challenge them to read this book and continue saying such things."
– Thomas Peters, American Papist, CatholicVote.org

"For anyone who wants to **defend the Church against unfair attacks** – or simply to separate the unfair attacks from those that are on target – this book is a **useful resource** ... His book makes a clear and documented case that the media coverage of the crisis has distorted public perceptions."
– Phil Lawler, CatholicCulture.org

"I **highly recommend** this book."
– Gus Lloyd, The Catholic Channel, Sirius/XM Radio

Catholic Priests Falsely Accused: The Facts, The Fraud, The Stories

"This is an important topic, and not just for priests and bishops! Everyone should be concerned about this. Please check out *Catholic Priests Falsely Accused: The Facts, The Fraud, The Stories*."
– Rev. John T. Zuhlsdorf ("Fr. Z"), "What Does The Prayer Really Say?", wdtprs.com

"David Pierre's *Catholic Priests Falsely Accused* is an important volume … [T]he author shows that legitimate outrage about abuse can at times boil over into wanton hysteria."
– Rev. Thomas G. Guarino, S.T.D., Professor of Systematic Theology, Seton Hall University

Made in the USA
San Bernardino, CA
02 February 2016